BLOODLINE

BLOODLINE

by Ernest J. Gaines

The Norton Library

W·W·NORTON & COMPANY·INC·

NEW YORK

For Dee with my deepest love

COPYRIGHT © 1963, 1964, 1968 BY ERNEST J. GAINES

First published in the Norton Library 1976
by arrangement with The Dial Press

ALL RIGHTS RESERVED
Published simultaneously in Canada
by George J. McLeod Limited, Toronto

Library of Congress Cataloging in Publication Data

Gaines, Ernest J. 1933-
  Bloodline.

  (The Norton Library)
  I. Title.
PZ4.G1422Bl7   [PS3537.A355]   813'.5'4   75-42393
ISBN 0-393-00798-7

Printed in the United States of America
3 4 5 6 7 8 9 0

Table of Contents

Acknowledgments

Acknowledgment is made to the following magazines where these stories first appeared: *Negro Digest* for "The Sky Is Gray"; *Sewanee Review* for "Just Like a Tree"; and *The Texas Quarterly* for an abbreviated version of "A Long Day in November."

A Long Day in November

A LONG DAY IN NOVEMBER

1: Somebody is shaking me but I dont want get up now, because I'm tired and I'm sleepy and I don't want get up now. It's warm under the cover here, but it's cold up there and I don't want get up now.

"Sonny?" I hear.

But I don't want get up, because it's cold up there. The cover is over my head and I'm under the sheet and the blanket and the quilt. It's warm under here and it's dark, because my eyes's shut. I keep my eyes shut because I don't want get up.

"Sonny?" I hear.

I don't know who's calling me, but it must be Mama because I'm home. I don't know who it is because I'm still asleep, but it must be Mama. She's shaking me by the foot. She's holding my ankle through the cover.

"Wake up, honey," she says.

But I don't want get up because it's cold up there and I don't want get cold. I try to go back to sleep, but she shakes my foot again.

"Hummm?" I say.

"Wake up, honey," I hear.

"Hummm?" I say.

"I want you get up and wee-wee," she says.

"I don't want wee-wee, Mama," I say.

"Come on," she says, shaking me. "Come on. Get up for Mama."

"It's cold up there," I say.

"Come on," she says. "Mama won't let her baby get cold."

I pull the sheet and blanket from under my head and push them back over my shoulder. I feel the cold and I try to cover up again, but Mama grabs the cover before I get it over me. Mama is standing 'side the bed and she's looking down at me, smiling. The room is dark. The lamp's on the mantelpiece, but it's kind of low. I see Mama's shadow on the wall over by Gran'mon's picture.

"I'm cold, Mama," I say.

"Mama go'n wrap his little coat round her baby," she says.

She goes over and get it off the chair where all my clothes's at, and I sit up in the bed. Mama brings the coat and put it on me, and she fastens some of the buttons.

"Now," she says. "See? You warm."

I gap' and look at Mama. She hugs me real hard and rubs her face against my face. My mama's face is warm and soft, and it feels good.

"I want my socks on," I say. "My feet go'n get cold on the floor."

Mama leans over and get my shoes from under the bed. She takes out my socks and slip them on my feet. I gap' and look at Mama pulling my socks up.

"Now," she says.

I get up but I can still feel that cold floor. I get on my knees and look under the bed for my pot.

"See it?" Mama says.

"Hanh?"

"See it under there?"

"Hanh?"

"I bet you didn't bring it in," she says. "Any time you sound like that you done forgot it."

"I left it on the chicken coop," I say.

"Well, go to the back door," Mama says. "Hurry up before you get cold."

I get off my knees and go back there, but it's too dark and I can't see. I come back where Mama's sitting on my bed.

"It's dark back there, Mama," I say. "I might trip over something."

Mama takes a deep breath and gets the lamp off the mantelpiece, and me and her go back in the kitchen. She unlatches the door, and I crack it open and the cold air comes in.

"Hurry," Mama says.

"All right."

I can see the fence back of the house and I can see the little pecan tree over by the toilet. I can see the big pecan tree over by the other fence by Miss Viola Brown's house. Miss Viola Brown must be sleeping because it's late at night. I bet you nobody else in the quarter's up now. I bet you I'm the only little boy up. They got plenty stars in the air, but I can't see the moon. There must be ain't no moon tonight. That grass is shining—and it must be done rained. That pecan tree's shadow's all over the back yard.

I get my tee-tee and I wee-wee. I wee-wee hard, because I don't want get cold. Mama latches the door when I get through wee-wee-ing.

"I want some water, Mama," I say.

"Let it out and put it right back in, huh?" Mama says.

She dips up some water and pours it in my cup, and I drink. I don't drink too much at once, because the water makes my teeth cold. I let my teeth warm up, and I drink some more.

"I got enough," I say.

5

Mama drinks the rest and then me and her go back in the front room.

"Sonny?" she says.

"Hanh?"

"Tomorrow morning when you get up me and you leaving here, hear?"

"Where we going?" I ask.

"We going to Gran'mon," Mama says.

"We leaving us house?" I ask.

"Yes," she says.

"Daddy leaving too?"

"No," she says. "Just me and you."

"Daddy don't want leave?"

"I don't know what your daddy wants," Mama says. "But for sure he don't want me. We leaving, hear?"

"Uh-huh," I say.

"I'm tired of it," Mama says.

"Hanh?"

"You won't understand, honey," Mama says. "You too young still."

"I'm getting cold, Mama," I say.

"All right," she says. She goes and put the lamp up, and comes back and sit on the bed 'side me. "Let me take your socks off," she says.

"I can take them off," I say.

Mama takes my coat off and I take my socks off. I get back in bed and Mama pulls the cover up over me. She leans over and kiss me on the jaw, and then she goes back to her bed. Mama's bed is over by the window. My bed is by the fireplace. I hear Mama get in the bed. I hear the spring, then I don't hear nothing because Mama's quiet. Then I hear Mama crying.

"Mama?" I call.

She don't answer me.

"Mama?" I call her.

"Go to sleep, baby," she says.

"You crying?" I ask.

"Go to sleep," Mama says.

"I don't want you to cry," I say.

"Mama's not crying," she says.

Then I don't hear nothing and I lay quiet, but I don't turn over because my spring'll make noise and I don't want make no noise because I want hear if my mama go'n cry again. I don't hear Mama no more and I feel warm in the bed and I pull the cover over my head and I feel good. I don't hear nothing no more and I feel myself going back to sleep.

Billy Joe Martin's got the tire and he's rolling it in the road, and I run to the gate to look at him. I want go out in the road, but Mama don't want me to play out there like Billy Joe Martin and the other children. . . . Lucy's playing 'side the house. She's jumping rope with—I don't know who that is. I go 'side the house and play with Lucy. Lucy beats me jumping rope. The rope keeps on hitting me on the leg. But it don't hit Lucy on the leg. Lucy jumps too high for it. . . . Me and Billy Joe Martin shoots marbles and I beat him shooting. . . . Mama's sweeping the gallery and knocking the dust out of the broom on the side of the house. Mama keeps on knocking the broom against the wall. Must be got plenty dust in the broom.

Somebody's beating on the door. Mama, somebody's beating on the door. Somebody's beating on the door, Mama.

"Amy, please let me in," I hear.

Somebody's beating on the door, Mama. Mama, somebody's beating on the door.

"Amy, honey; honey, please let me in."

I push the cover back and I listen. I hear Daddy beating on the door.

"Mama?" I say. "Mama, Daddy's knocking on the door. He want come in."

"Go back to sleep, Sonny," Mama says.

7

"Daddy's out there," I say. "He want come in."

"Go back to sleep, I told you," Mama says.

I lay back on my pillow and listen.

"Amy," Daddy says, "I know you woke. Open the door."

Mama don't answer him.

"Amy, honey," Daddy says. "My sweet dumpling, let me in. It's freezing out here."

Mama still won't answer Daddy.

"Mama?" I say.

"Go back to sleep, Sonny," she says.

"Mama, Daddy want come in," I say.

"Let him crawl through the key hole," Mama says.

It gets quiet after this, and it stays quiet a little while, and then Daddy says:

"Sonny?"

"Hanh?"

"Come open the door for your daddy."

"Mama go'n whip me if I get up," I say.

"I won't let her whip you," Daddy says. "Come and open the door like a good boy."

I push the cover back and I sit up in the bed and look over at Mama's bed. Mama's under the cover and she's quiet like she's asleep. I get on the floor and get my socks out of my shoes. I get back in the bed and slip them on, and then I go and unlatch the door for Daddy. Daddy comes in and rubs my head with his hand. His hand is hard and cold.

"Look what I brought you and your mama," he says.

"What?" I ask.

Daddy takes a paper bag out of his jumper pocket.

"Candy?" I say.

"Uh-huh."

Daddy opens the bag and I stick my hand in there and take a whole handful. Daddy wraps the bag up again and sticks it in his pocket.

"Get back in that bed, Sonny," Mama says.

"I'm eating candy," I say.

"Get back in that bed like I told you," Mama says.

"Daddy's up with me," I say.

"You heard me, boy?"

"You can take your candy with you," Daddy says. "Get back in the bed."

He follows me to the bed and tucks the cover under me. I lay in the bed and eat my candy. The candy is hard, and I sound just like Paul eating corn. I bet you little old Paul is some cold out there in that back yard. I hope he ain't laying in that water like he always do. I bet you he'll freeze in that water in all this cold. I'm sure glad I ain't a pig. They ain't got no mama and no daddy and no house.

I hear the spring when Daddy gets in the bed.

"Honey?" Daddy says.

Mama don't answer him.

"Honey?" he says.

Mama must be gone back to sleep, because she don't answer him.

"Honey?" Daddy says.

"Get your hands off me," Mama says.

"Honey, you know I can't keep my hands off you," Daddy says.

"Well, just do," Mama says.

"Honey, you don't mean that," Daddy says. "You know 'fore God you don't mean that. Come on, say you don't mean it. I can't shut these eyes till you say you don't mean it."

"Don't touch me," Mama says.

"Honey," Daddy says. Then he starts crying. "Honey, please."

Daddy cries a good little while, and then he stops. I don't chew on my candy while Daddy's crying, but when he stops I chew on another piece.

9

"Go to sleep, Sonny," he says.

"I want eat my candy," I say.

"Hurry then. You got to go to school tomorrow."

I put another piece in my mouth and chew on it.

"Honey?" I hear Daddy saying. "Honey, you go'n wake me up to go to work?"

"I do hope you stop bothering me," Mama says.

"Wake me up round four thirty, hear, honey?" Daddy says. "I can cut 'bout six tons tomorrow. Maybe seven."

Mama don't say nothing to Daddy, and I feel sleepy again. I finish chewing my last piece of candy and I turn on my side. I feel good because the bed is warm. But I still got my socks on.

"Daddy?" I call.

"Go to sleep," Daddy says.

"My socks still on," I say.

"Let them stay on tonight," Daddy says. "Go to sleep."

"My feet don't feel good in socks," I say.

"Please go to sleep, Sonny," Daddy says. "I got to get up at four thirty, and it's hitting close to two now."

I don't say nothing, but I don't like to sleep with my socks on. But I stay quiet. Daddy and Mama don't say nothing, either, and little bit later I hear Daddy snoring. I feel drowsy myself.

I run around the house in the mud because it done rained and I feel the mud between my toes. The mud is soft and I like to play in it. I try to get out the mud, but I can't get out. I'm not stuck in the mud, but I can't get out. Lucy can't come over and play in the mud because her mama don't want her to catch cold. . . . Billy Joe Martin shows me his dime and puts it back in his pocket. Mama bought me a pretty little red coat and I show it to Lucy. But I don't let Billy Joe Martin put his hand on it. Lucy can touch it all she wants, but I don't let Billy Joe Martin put his hand on it. . . . Me and Lucy get on the horse and ride up and down the road. The horse runs fast, and me and Lucy bounce on the horse and laugh. . . . Mama and Daddy and Uncle Al and Gran'-mon's sitting by the fire talking. I'm outside shooting marbles, but I hear them. I don't know what they talking about, but I hear them. I hear them. I hear them. I hear them.

I don't want wake up, but I'm waking up. Mama and Daddy's talking. I want go back to sleep, but they talking too loud. I feel my foot in the sock. I don't like socks on when I'm in the bed. I want go back to sleep, but I can't. Mama and Daddy talking too much.

"Honey, you let me oversleep," Daddy says. "Look here, it's going on seven o'clock."

"You ought to been thought about that last night," Mama says.

"Honey, please," Daddy says. "Don't start a fuss right off this morning."

"Then don't open your mouth," Mama says.

"Honey, the car broke down," Daddy says. "What I was suppose to do, it broke down on me. I just couldn't walk away and not try to fix it."

Mama's quiet.

"Honey," Daddy says, "don't be mad with me. Come on, now."

"Don't touch me," Mama says.

"Honey, I got to go to work. Come on."

"I mean it," she says.

"Honey, how can I work without touching you? You know I can't do a day's work without touching you some."

"I told you not to put your hands on me," Mama says. I hear her slap Daddy on the hand. "I mean it," she says.

"Honey," Daddy says, "this is Eddie, your husband."

"Go back to your car," Mama says. "Go rub against it. You ought to be able to find a hole in it somewhere."

"Honey, you oughtn't talk like that in the house," Daddy says. "What if Sonny hear you?"

I stay quiet and I don't move because I don't want them to know I'm woke.

"Honey, listen to me," Daddy says. "From the bottom of my heart I'm sorry. Now, come on."

"I told you once," Mama says, "you not getting on me. Go get on your car."

"Honey, respect the child," Daddy says.

"How come you don't respect him?" Mama says. "How come you don't come home sometime and respect him? How come you don't leave that car alone and come home and respect him? How come you don't respect him? You the one need to respect him."

"I told you it broke down," Daddy says. "I was coming home when it broke down on me. I even had to leave it out on the road. I made it here quick as I could."

"You can go back quick as you can, for all I care," Mama says.

"Honey, you don't mean that," Daddy says. "I know you don't mean that. You just saying that because you mad."

"Just don't touch me," Mama says.

"Honey, I got to get out and make some bread for us," Daddy says.

"Get out if you want," Mama says. "They got a jailhouse for them who don't support their family."

"Honey, please don't talk about a jail," Daddy says. "It's too cold. You don't know how cold it is in a jailhouse this time of the year."

Mama's quiet.

"Honey?" Daddy says.

"I hope you let me go back to sleep," Mama says. "Please."

"Honey, don't go back to sleep on me," Daddy says. "Honey—"

"I'm getting up," Mama says. "Damn all this."

I hear the springs mash down on the bed boards. My head's under the cover, but I can just see Mama pushing the cover down the bed. Then I hear her walking across the floor and going back in the kitchen.

"Oh, Lord," Daddy says. "Oh, Lord. The suffering a man got to go through in this world. Sonny?" he says.

"Don't wake that baby up," Mama says, from the door.

"I got to have somebody to talk to," Daddy says. "Sonny?"

"I told you not to wake him up," Mama says.

"You don't want talk to me," Daddy says. "I need somebody to talk to. Sonny?" he says.

"Hanh?"

"See what you did?" Mama says. "You woke him up, and he ain't going back to sleep."

Daddy comes across the floor and sits down on the side of the bed. He looks down at me and passes his hand over my face.

"You love your daddy, Sonny?" he says.

"Uh-huh."

"Please love me," Daddy says.

I look up at Daddy and he looks at me, and then he just falls down on me and starts crying.

"A man needs somebody to love him," he says.

"Get love from what you give love," Mama says, back in the kitchen. "You love your car. Go let it love you back."

Daddy shakes his face in the cover.

"The suffering a man got to go through in this world," he says. "Sonny, I hope you never have to go through all this."

Daddy lays there 'side me a long time. I can hear Mama back in the kitchen. I hear her putting some wood in the stove, and then I hear her lighting the fire. I hear her pouring water in the tea kettle, and I hear when she sets the kettle on the stove.

13

Daddy raises up and wipes his eyes. He looks at me and shakes his head, then he goes and puts his overalls on.

"It's a hard life," he says. "Hard, hard. One day, Sonny—you too young right now—but one day you'll know what I mean."

"Can I get up, Daddy?"

"Better ask your mama," Daddy says.

"Can I get up, Mama?" I call.

Mama don't answer me.

"Mama?" I call.

"Your paw standing in there," Mama says. "He the one woke you up."

"Can I get up, Daddy?"

"Sonny, I got enough troubles right now," Daddy say.

"I want get up and wee-wee," I say.

"Get up," Mama says. "You go'n worry me till I let you get up anyhow."

I crawl from under the cover and look at my feet. I got just one sock on and I look for the other one under the cover. I find it and slip it on and then I get on the floor. But that floor is still cold. I hurry up and put on my clothes, and I get my shoes and go and sit on the bed to put them on.

Daddy waits till I finish tying up my shoes, and me and him go back in the kitchen. I get in the corner 'side the stove and Daddy comes over and stands 'side me. The fire is warm and it feels good.

Mama is frying salt meat in the skillet. The skillet's over one hole and the tea kettle's over the other one. The water's boiling and the tea kettle is whistling. I look at the steam shooting up to the loft.

Mama goes outside and gets my pot. She holds my pot for me and I wee-wee in it. Then Mama carries my pot in the front room and puts it under my bed.

Daddy pours some water in the wash basin and washes his face, and then he washes my face. He dumps the water out the back door, and me and him sit at the table. Mama brings the food to the table. She stands over me till I get through saying my blessing, and then she goes back to the stove. Me and Daddy eat.

"You love your daddy?" he says.

"Uh-huh," I say.

"That's a good boy," he says. "Always love your daddy."

"I love Mama, too. I love her more than I love you."

"You got a good mama," Daddy says. "I love her, too. She the only thing keep me going—'cluding you, too."

I look at Mama standing 'side the stove, warming.

"Why don't you come to the table and eat with us," Daddy says.

"I'm not hungry," Mama says.

"I'm sorry, baby," Daddy says. "I mean it."

Mama just looks down at the stove and don't answer Daddy.

"You got a right to be mad," Daddy says. "I ain't nothing but a' old rotten dog."

Daddy eats his food and looks at me across the table. I pick up a piece of meat and chew on it. I like the skin because the skin is hard. I keep the skin a long time.

"Well, I better get going," Daddy says. "Maybe if I work hard I'll get me a couple tons."

Daddy gets up from the table and goes in the front room. He comes back with his jumper and his hat on. Daddy's hat is gray and it got a hole on the side.

"I'm leaving, honey," he tells Mama.

Mama don't answer Daddy.

"Honey, tell me ' 'Bye, old dog,' or something," Daddy says. "Just don't stand there."

Mama still don't answer him, and Daddy jerks his cane knife out the wall and goes on out. I chew on my meat skin. I like it because it's hard.

"Hurry up, honey," Mama says. "We going to Mama."

Mama goes in the front room and I stay at the table and eat. I finish eating and I go in the front room where Mama is. Mama's pulling a big bundle of clothes from under the bed.

"What's that, Mama?" I ask.

"Us clothes," she says.

"We go'n take us clothes down to Gran'mon?"

"I'm go'n try," Mama says. "Find your cap and put it on."

I see my cap hanging on the chair and I put it on and fasten the strap under my chin. Mama fixes my shirt in my pants, and then she goes and puts on her overcoat. Her overcoat is black and her hat is black. She puts on her hat and looks in the looking glass. I can see her face in the glass. Look like she want cry. She comes from the dresser and looks at the big bundle of clothes on the floor.

"Where's your pot?" she says. "Find it."

I get my pot from under the bed.

"Still got some wee-wee in it," I say.

"Go to the back door and dump it out," Mama says.

I go back in the kitchen and open the door. It's cold out there, and I can see the frost all over the grass. The grass is white with frost. I dump the wee-wee out and come back in the front.

"Come on," Mama says.

She drags the big bundle of clothes out on the gallery and I shut the door. Mama squats down and puts the bundle on her head, and then she stands up and me and her go down the steps. Soon's I get out in the road I can feel the wind. It's strong and it's blowing in my face. My face is cold and one of my hands is cold.

It's red over there back of the trees. Mr. Guerin's house is over there. I see Mr. Guerin's big old dog. He must be don't see me and Mama because he ain't barking at us.

16

"Don't linger back too far," Mama says.

I run and catch up with Mama. Me and Mama's the only two people walking in the road now.

I look up and I see the tree in Gran'mon's yard. We go little farther and I see the house. I run up ahead of Mama and hold the gate open for her. After she goes in I let the gate slam.

Spot starts barking soon's he sees me. He runs down the steps at me and I let him smell my pot. Spot follows me and Mama back to the house.

"Gran'mon?" I call.

"Who that out there?" Gran'mon asks.

"Me," I say.

"What you doing out there in all that cold for, boy?" Gran'mon says. I hear Gran'mon coming to the door fussing. She opens the door and looks at me and Mama.

"What you doing here with all that?" she asks.

"I'm leaving him, Mama," Mama says.

"Eddie?" Gran'mon says. "What he done you now?"

"I'm just tired of it," Mama says.

"Come in here out that cold," Gran'mon says. "Walking out there in all that weather . . ."

We go inside and Mama drops the big bundle of clothes on the floor. I go to the fire and warm my hands. Mama and Gran'mon come to the fire and Mama stands at the other end of the fireplace and warms her hands.

"Now what that no good nigger done done?" Gran'mon asks.

"Mama, I'm just tired of Eddie running up and down the road in that car," Mama says.

"He beat you?" Gran'mon asks.

"No, he didn't beat me," Mama says. "Mama, Eddie didn't get home till after two this morning. Messing around with that old car somewhere out on the road all night."

"I told you," Gran'mon says. "I told you when that nigger got that car that was go'n happen. I told you. No—you wouldn't listen. I told you. Put a fool in a car and he becomes a bigger fool. Where that yellow thing at now?"

"God telling," Mama says. "He left with his cane knife."

"I warned you 'bout that nigger," Gran'mon says. "Even 'fore you married him. I sung at you and sung at you. I said, 'Amy, that nigger ain't no good. A yellow nigger with a gap like that 'tween his front teeth ain't no good.' But you wouldn't listen."

"Can me and Sonny stay here?" Mama asks.

"Where else can y'all go?" Gran'mon says. "I'm your mon, ain't I? You think I can put you out in the cold like he did?"

"He didn't put me out, Mama, I left," Mama says.

"You finally getting some sense in your head," Gran'mon says. "You ought to been left that nigger years ago."

Uncle Al comes in the front room and looks at the bundle of clothes on the floor. Uncle Al's got on his overalls and got just one strap hooked. The other strap's hanging down his back.

"Fix that thing on you," Gran'mon says. "You not in a stable."

Uncle Al fixes his clothes and looks at me and Mama at the fire.

"Y'all had a round?" he asks Mama.

"Eddie and that car again," Mama says.

"That's all they want these days," Gran'mon says. "Cars. Why don't they marry them cars? No. When they got their troubles, they come running to the womenfolks. When they ain't got no troubles and when their pockets full of money they run jump in the car. I told you that when you was working to help him get that car."

Uncle Al stands 'side me at the fireplace, and I lean

against him and look at the steam coming out a piece of wood. Lord knows I get tired of Gran'mon fussing all the time.

"Y'all moving in with us?" Uncle Al asks.

"For a few days," Mama says. "Then I'll try to find another place somewhere in the quarter."

"We got plenty room here," Uncle Al says. "This old man here can sleep with me."

Uncle Al gets a little stick out of the corner and hands it to me so I can light it for him. I hold it to the fire till it's lit, and I hand it back to Uncle Al. Uncle Al turns the pipe upside down in his mouth and holds the fire to it. When the pipe's good and lit, Uncle Al gives me the little stick and I throw it back in the fire.

"Y'all ate anything?" Gran'mon asks.

"Sonny ate," Mama says. "I'm not hungry."

"I reckon you go'n start looking for work now?" Gran'mon says.

"There's plenty cane to cut," Mama says. "I'll get me a cane knife and go out tomorrow morning."

"Out in all that cold?" Gran'mon says.

"They got plenty women cutting cane," Mama says. "I don't mind. I done it before."

"You used to be such a pretty little thing, Amy," Gran'mon says. "Long silky curls. Prettiest little face on this whole plantation. You could've married somebody worth something. But, no, you had to go throw yourself away to that yellow nigger who don't care for nobody, 'cluding himself."

"I loved Eddie," Mama says.

"Poot," Gran'mon says.

"He wasn't like this when we married," Mama says.

"Every nigger from Bayonne like this now, then, and forever," Gran'mon says.

"Not then," Mama says. "He was the sweetest person . . ."

"And you fell for him?" Gran'mon says.

". . . He changed after he got that car," Mama says. "He changed overnight."

"Well, you learned your lesson," Gran'mon says. "We all get teached something no matter how old we get. 'Live and learn,' what they say."

"Eddie's all right," Uncle Al says. "He—"

"You keep out of this, Albert," Gran'mon says. "It don't concern you."

Uncle Al don't say no more, and I can feel his hand on my shoulder. I like Uncle Al because he's good, and he never talk bad about Daddy. But Gran'mon's always talking bad about Daddy.

"Freddie's still there," Gran'mon says.

"Mama, please," Mama says.

"Why not?" Gran'mon says. "He always loved you."

"Not in front of him," Mama says.

Mama leaves the fireplace and goes to the bundle of clothes. I can hear her untying the bundle.

"Ain't it 'bout time you was leaving for school?" Uncle Al asks.

"I don't want go," I say. "It's too cold."

"It's never too cold for school," Mama says. "Warm up good and let Uncle Al button your coat for you."

I get closer to the fire and I feel the fire hot on my pants. I turn around and warm my back. I turn again, and Uncle Al leans over and buttons up my coat. Uncle Al's pipe almost gets in my face, and it don't smell good.

"Now," Uncle Al says. "You all ready to go. You want take a potato with you?"

"Uh-huh."

Uncle Al leans over and gets me a potato out of the ashes. He knocks all the ashes off and puts the potato in my pocket.

"Wait," Mama says. "Mama, don't you have a little paper bag?"

Gran'mon looks on the mantelpiece and gets a paper bag. There's something in the bag, and she takes it out and hands the bag to Mama. Mama puts the potato in the bag and puts it in my pocket. Then she goes and gets my book and tucks it under my arm.

"Now you ready," she says. "And remember, when you get out for dinner come back here. Don't you forget and go up home now. You hear, Sonny?"

"Uh-huh."

"Come on," Uncle Al says. "I'll open the gate for you."

" 'Bye, Mama," I say.

"Be a good boy," Mama says. "Eat your potato at recess. Don't eat it in class now."

Me and Uncle Al go out on the gallery. The sun is shining but it's still cold out there. Spot follows me and Uncle Al down the walk. Uncle Al opens the gate for me and I go out in the road. I hate to leave Uncle Al and Spot. And I hate to leave Mama—and I hate to leave the fire. But I got to, because they want me to learn.

"See you at twelve," Uncle Al says.

I go up the quarter and Uncle Al and Spot go back to the house. I see all the children going to school. But I don't see Lucy. When I get to her house I'm go'n stop at the gate and call her. She must be don't want go to school, cold as it is.

It still got some ice in the water. I better not walk in the water. I'll get my feet wet and Mama'll whip me.

When I get closer I look and I see Lucy and her mama on the gallery. Lucy's mama ties her bonnet for her, and Lucy comes down the steps. She runs down the walk toward the gate. Lucy's bonnet is red and her coat is red.

"Hi," I say.

"Hi," she says.

"It's some cold," I say.

"Unnn-hunnnn," Lucy says.

Me and Lucy walk side by side up the quarter. Lucy's got her book in her book sack.

"We moved," I say. "We staying with Gran'mon now."

"Y'all moved?" Lucy asks.

"Uh-huh."

"Y'all didn't move," Lucy says. "When y'all moved?"

"This morning."

"Who moved y'all?" Lucy asks.

"Me and Mama," I say. "I'm go'n sleep with Uncle Al."

"My legs getting cold," Lucy says.

"I got a potato," I say. "In my pocket."

"You go'n eat it and give me piece?" Lucy says.

"Uh-huh," I say. "At recess."

Me and Lucy walk up the quarter, and Lucy stops and touches the ice with her shoe.

"You go'n get your foot wet," I say.

"No, I'm not," Lucy says.

Lucy breaks the ice with her shoe and laughs. I laugh and I break a piece of ice with my shoe. Me and Lucy laugh and I see the smoke coming out of Lucy's mouth. I open my mouth and go, "Haaaa," and plenty smoke comes out of my mouth. Lucy laughs and points at the smoke.

Me and Lucy go on up the quarter to the schoolhouse. Billy Joe Martin and Ju-Ju and them's playing marbles right by the gate. Over 'side the schoolhouse Shirley and Dottie and Katie's jumping rope. On the other side of the schoolhouse some more children playing "Patty-cake, patty-cake, baker-man" to keep warm. Lucy goes where Shirley and them's jumping rope and asks them to play. I stop where Billy Joe Martin and them's at and watch them shoot marbles.

2: It's warm inside the schoolhouse. Bill made a big fire in the heater, and I can hear it roaring up the pipes. I look out the window and I can see the smoke flying across the yard. Bill sure knows how to make a good fire. Bill's the biggest boy in school, and he always makes the fire for us.

Everybody's studying their lesson, but I don't know mine. I wish I knowed it, but I don't. Mama didn't teach me my lesson last night, and she didn't teach it to me this morning, and I don't know it.

"Bob and Rex in the yard. Rex is barking at the cow." I don't know what all this other reading is. I see "Rex" again, and I see "cow" again—but I don't know what all the rest of it is.

Bill comes up to the heater and I look up and see him putting another piece of wood in the fire. He goes back to his seat and sits down 'side Juanita. Miss Hebert looks at Bill when he goes back to his seat. I look in my book at Bob and Rex. Bob's got on a white shirt and blue pants. Rex is a German police dog. He's white and brown. Mr. Bouie's got a dog just like Rex. He don't bite though. He's a good dog. But Mr. Guerin's old dog'll bite you for sure. I seen him this morning when me and Mama was going down to Gran'mon's house.

I ain't go'n eat dinner at us house because me and Mama don't stay there no more. I'm go'n eat at Gran'mon's house. I don't know where Daddy go'n eat dinner. He must be go'n cook his own dinner.

I can hear Bill and Juanita back of me. They whispering to each other, but I can hear them. Juanita's some pretty. I hope I was big so I could love her. But I better look at my lesson and don't think about other things.

"First grade," Miss Hebert says.

We go up to the front and sit down on the bench. Miss

Hebert looks at us and make a mark in her roll book. She puts the roll book down and comes over to the bench where we at.

"Does everyone know his lesson today?" she asks.

"Yes, Ma'am," Lucy says, louder than anybody else in the whole schoolhouse.

"Good," Miss Hebert says. "And I'll start with you today, Lucy. Hold your book in one hand and begin."

" 'Bob and Rex are in the yard,' " Lucy reads. " 'Rex is barking at the cow. The cow is watching Rex.' "

"Good," Miss Hebert says. "Point to barking."

Lucy points.

"Good. Now point to watching."

Lucy points again.

"Good," Miss Hebert says. "Shirley Ann, let's see how well you can read."

I look in the book at Bob and Rex. "Rex is barking at the cow. The cow is looking at Rex."

"William Joseph," Miss Hebert says.

I'm next, I'm scared. I don't know my lesson and Miss Hebert go'n whip me. Miss Hebert don't like you when you don't know your lesson. I can see her strap over there on the table. I can see the clock and the little bell, too. Bill split the end of the strap, and them little ends sting some. Soon 's Billy Joe Martin finishes, then it's me. I don't know . . . Mama ought to been . . . "Bob and Rex" . . .

"Eddie," Miss Hebert says.

I don't know my lesson. I don't know my lesson. I don't know my lesson. I feel warm. I'm wet. I hear the wee-wee dripping on the floor. I'm crying. I'm crying because I wee-wee on myself. My clothes's wet. Lucy and them go'n laugh at me. Billy Joe Martin and them go'n tease me. I don't know my lesson. I don't know my lesson. I don't know my lesson.

"Oh, Eddie, look what you've done," I think I hear Miss Hebert saying. I don't know if she's saying this, but I think I hear her say it. My eyes's shut and I'm crying. I don't want look at none of them, because I know they laughing at me.

"It's running under that bench there now," Billy Joe Martin says. "Look out for your feet back there, it's moving fast."

"William Joseph," Miss Hebert says. "Go over there and stand in that corner. Turn your face to the wall and stay there until I tell you to move."

I hear Billy Joe Martin leaving the bench, and then it's quiet. But I don't open my eyes.

"Eddie," Miss Hebert says, "go stand by the heater."

I don't move, because I'll see them, and I don't want see them.

"Eddie?" Miss Hebert says.

But I don't answer her, and I don't move.

"Bill?" Miss Hebert says.

I hear Bill coming up to the front and then I feel him taking me by the hand and leading me away. I walk with my eyes shut. Me and Bill stop at the heater, because I can feel the fire. Then Bill takes my book and leaves me standing there.

"Juanita," Miss Hebert says, "get a mop, will you, please."

I hear Juanita going to the back, and then I hear her coming back to the front. The fire pops in the heater, but I don't open my eyes. Nobody's saying anything, but I know they all watching me.

When Juanita gets through mopping up the wee-wee she carries the mop back to the closet, and I hear Miss Hebert going on with the lesson. When she gets through with the first graders, she calls the second graders up there.

Bill comes up to the heater and puts another piece of wood in the fire.

"Want turn around?" he asks me.

I don't answer him, but I got my eyes open now and I'm looking down at the floor. Bill turns me round so I can dry

25

the back of my pants. He pats me on the shoulder and goes back to his seat.

After Miss Hebert gets through with the second graders, she tells the children they can go out for recess. I can hear them getting their coats and hats. When they all leave I raise my head. I still see Bill and Juanita and Veta sitting there. Bill smiles at me, but I don't smile back. My clothes's dry now, and I feel better. I know the rest of the children go'n tease me, though.

"Bill, why don't you and the rest of the seventh graders put your arithmetic problems on the board," Miss Hebert says. "We'll look at them after recess."

Bill and them stand up, and I watch them go to the blackboard in the back.

"Eddie?" Miss Hebert says.

I turn and I see her sitting behind her desk. And I see Billy Joe Martin standing in the corner with his face to the wall.

"Come up to the front," Miss Hebert says.

I go up there looking down at the floor, because I know she go'n whip me now.

"William Joseph, you may leave," Miss Hebert says.

Billy Joe Martin runs over and gets his coat, and then he runs outside to shoot marbles. I stand in front of Miss Hebert's desk with my head down.

"Look up," she says.

I raise my head and look at Miss Hebert. She's smiling, and she don't look mad.

"Now," she says. "Did you study your lesson last night?"

"Yes, ma'am," I say.

"I want the truth, now," she says. "Did you?"

It's a sin to story in the churchhouse, but I'm scared Miss Hebert go'n whip me.

"Yes, ma'am," I say.

"Did you study it this morning?" she asks.

"Yes, ma'am," I say.

"Then why didn't you know it?" she asks.

I feel a big knot coming up in my throat and I feel like I'm go'n cry again. I'm scared Miss Hebert go'n whip me, that's why I story to her.

"You didn't study your lesson, did you?" she says.

I shake my head. "No, ma'am."

"You didn't study it last night either, did you?"

"No, ma'am," I say. "Mama didn't have time to help me. Daddy wasn't home. Mama didn't have time to help me."

"Where is your father?" Miss Hebert asks.

"Cutting cane."

"Here on this place?"

"Yes, ma'am," I say.

Miss Hebert looks at me, and then she gets out a pencil and starts writing on a piece of paper. I look at her writing and I look at the clock and the strap. I can hear the clock. I can hear Billy Joe Martin and them shooting marbles outside. I can hear Lucy and them jumping rope, and some more children playing "Patty-cake."

"I want you to give this to your mother or your father when you get home," Miss Hebert says. "This is only a little note saying I would like to see them sometime when they aren't too busy."

"We don't live home no more," I say.

"Oh?" Miss Hebert says. "Did you move?"

"Me and Mama," I say. "But Daddy didn't."

Miss Hebert looks at me, and then she writes some more on the note. She puts her pencil down and folds the note up.

"Be sure to give this to your mother," she says. "Put it in your pocket and don't lose it."

I take the note from Miss Hebert, but I don't leave the desk.

"Do you want to go outside?" she asks.

"Yes, ma'am."

"You may leave," she says.

I go over and get my coat and cap, and then I go out in the yard. I see Billy Joe Martin and Charles and them shooting marbles over by the gate. I don't go over there because they'll tease me. I go 'side the schoolhouse and look at Lucy and them jumping rope. Lucy ain't jumping right now.

"Hi, Lucy," I say.

Lucy looks over at Shirley and they laugh. They look at my pants and laugh.

"You want a piece of potato?" I ask Lucy.

"No," Lucy says. "And you not my boyfriend no more, either."

I look at Lucy and I go stand 'side the wall in the sun. I peel my potato and eat it. And look like soon 's I get through, Miss Hebert comes to the front and says recess is over.

We go back inside, and I go to the back and take off my coat and cap. Bill comes back there and hang the things up for us. I go over to Miss Hebert's desk and Miss Hebert gives me my book. I go back to my seat and sit down 'side Lucy.

"Hi, Lucy," I say.

Lucy looks at Shirley and Shirley puts her hand over her mouth and laughs. I feel like getting up from there and socking Shirley in the mouth, but I know Miss Hebert'll whip me. Because I got no business socking people after I done wee-wee on myself. I open my book and look at my lesson so I don't have to look at none of them.

3: It's almost dinner time, and when I get home I ain't coming back here either, now. I'm go'n stay there. I'm go'n stay right there and sit by the fire. Lucy and them don't want play with me, and I ain't coming back up here. Miss Hebert go'n touch that little bell in a little while. She getting ready to touch it right now.

Soon 's Miss Hebert touches the bell all the children run go get their hats and coats. I unhook my coat and drop it on the bench till I put my cap on. Then I put my coat on, and I get my book and leave.

I see Bill and Juanita going out the schoolyard, and I run and catch up with them. Time I get there I hear Billy Joe Martin and them coming up behind us.

"Look at that baby," Billy Joe Martin says.

"Piss on himself," Ju-Ju says.

"Y'all leave him alone," Bill says.

"Baby, baby, piss on himself," Billy Joe Martin sings.

"What did I say now?" Bill says.

"Piss on himself," Billy Joe Martin says.

"Wait," Bill says. "Let me take off my belt."

"Good-bye, piss pot," Billy Joe Martin says. Him and Ju-Ju run down the road. They spank their hind parts with their hands and run like horses.

"They just bad," Juanita says.

"Don't pay them no mind," Bill says. "They'll leave you alone."

We go on down the quarter and Bill and Juanita hold hands. I go to Gran'mon's gate and open it. I look at Bill and Juanita going down the quarter. They walking close together, and Juanita done put her head on Bill's shoulder. I like to see Bill and Juanita like that. It makes me feel good. But I go in the yard and I don't feel good any more. I know old Gran'mon go'n start her fussing. Lord in Heaven knows I get tired of all this fussing, day and night. Spot runs down the walk to meet me. I put my hand on his head and me and him go back to the gallery. I make him stay on the gallery, because Gran'mon don't want him inside. I pull the door open and I see Gran'mon and Uncle Al sitting by the fire. I look for my mama, but I don't see her.

"Where Mama?" I ask Uncle Al.

"In the kitchen," Gran'mon says. "But she talking to somebody."

I go back to the kitchen.

"Come back here," Gran'mon says.

"I want see my mama," I say.

"You'll see her when she come out," Gran'mon says.

"I want see my mama now," I say.

"Don't you hear me talking to you, boy?" Gran'mon hollers.

"What's the matter?" Mama asks. Mama comes out of the kitchen and Mr. Freddie Jackson comes out of there, too. I hate Mr. Freddie Jackson. I never did like him. He always want to be round my mama.

"That boy don't listen to nobody," Gran'mon says.

"Hi, Sonny," Mr. Freddie Jackson says.

I look at him standing there, but I don't speak to him. I take the note out of my pocket and hand it to my mama.

"What's this?" Mama says.

"Miss Hebert sent it."

Mama unfolds the note and take it to the fireplace to read it. I can see her mouth working. When she gets through reading, she folds the note up again.

"She want see me or Eddie sometime when we free," Mama says. "Sonny been doing pretty bad in his class."

"I can just see that nigger husband of yours in a schoolhouse," Gran'mon says. "I doubt if he ever went to one."

"Mama, please," Mama says.

Mama helps me off with my coat and I go to the fireplace and stand 'side Uncle Al. Uncle Al pulls me between his legs and he holds my hand out to the fire.

"Well?" I hear Gran'mon saying.

"You know how I feel 'bout her," Mr. Freddie Jackson says. "My house opened to her and Sonny any time she want come there."

"Well?" Gran'mon says.

"Mama, I'm still married to Eddie," Mama says.

"You mean you still love that yellow thing," Gran'mon says. "That's what you mean, ain't it?"

"I didn't say that," Mama says. "What would people say, out one house and in another one the same day?"

"Who care what people say?" Gran'mon says. "Let people say what they big enough to say. You looking out for yourself, not what people say."

"You understand, don't you, Freddie?" Mama says.

"I think I do," he says. "But like I say, Amy, any time— you know that."

"And there ain't no time like right now," Gran'mon says. "You can take that bundle of clothes down there for her."

"Let her make up her own mind, Rachel," Uncle Al says. "She can make up her own mind."

"If you know what's good for you you better keep out of this," Gran'mon says. "She my daughter and if she ain't got sense enough to look out for herself, I have. What you want to do, go out in that field cutting cane in the morning?"

"I don't mind it," Mama says.

"You done forgot how hard cutting cane is?" Gran'mon says. "You must be done forgot."

"I ain't forgot," Mama says. "But if the other women can do it, I suppose I can do it, too."

"Now you talking back," Gran'mon says.

"I'm not talking back, Mama," Mama says. "I just feel it ain't right to leave one house and go to another house the same day. That ain't right in nobody's book."

"Maybe she's right, Mrs. Rachel," Mr. Freddie Jackson says.

"Her trouble is she's still in love with that mariny," Gran'mon says. "That's what your trouble is. You ain't satisfied 'less he got you doing all the work while he rip and run

31

up and down the road with his other nigger friends. No, you ain't satisfied."

Gran'mon goes back in the kitchen fussing. After she leaves the fire, everything gets quiet. Everything stays quiet a minute, and then Gran'mon starts singing back in the kitchen.

"Why did you bring your book home?" Mama says.

"Miss Hebert say I can stay home if I want," I say. "We had us lesson already."

"You sure she said that?" Mama says.

"Uh-huh."

"I'm go'n ask her, you know."

"She said it," I say.

Mama don't say no more, but I know she still looking at me, but I don't look at her. Then Spot starts barking outside and everybody look that way. But nobody don't move. Spot keeps on barking, and I go to the door to see what he's barking at. I see Daddy coming up the walk. I pull the door and go back to the fireplace.

"Daddy coming, Mama," I say.

"Wait," Gran'mon says, coming out the kitchen. "Let me talk to that nigger. I'll give him a piece of my mind."

Gran'mon goes to the door and pushes it open. She stands in the door and I hear Daddy talking to Spot. Then Daddy comes up to the gallery.

"Amy in there, Mama?" Daddy says.

"She is," Gran'mon says.

I hear Daddy coming up the steps.

"And where you think you going?" Gran'mon asks.

"I want speak to her," Daddy says.

"Well, she don't want speak to you," Gran'mon says. "So you might 's well go right on back down them steps and march right straight out of my yard."

"I want speak to my wife," Daddy says.

"She ain't your wife no more," Gran'mon says. "She left you."

"What you mean she left me?" Daddy says.

"She ain't up at your house no more, is she?" Gran'mon says. "That look like a good enough sign to me that she done left."

"Amy?" Daddy calls.

Mama don't answer him. She's looking down in the fire. I don't feel good when Mama's looking like that.

"Amy?" Daddy calls.

Mama still don't answer him.

"You satisfied?" Gran'mon says.

"You the one trying to make Amy leave me," Daddy says. "You ain't never liked me—from the starting."

"That's right, I never did," Gran'mon says. "You yellow, you got a gap 'tween your teeth, and you ain't no good. You want me to say more?"

"You always wanted her to marry somebody else," Daddy says.

"You right again," Gran'mon says.

"Amy?" Daddy calls. "Can you hear me, honey?"

"She can hear you," Gran'mon says. "She's standing right there by that fireplace. She can hear you good 's I can hear you, and nigger, I can hear you too good for comfort."

"I'm going in there," Daddy says. "She got somebody in there and I'm going in there and see."

"You just take one more step toward my door," Gran'mon says, "and it'll take a' undertaker to get you out of here. So help me, God, I'll get that butcher knife out of that kitchen and chop on your tail till I can't see tail to chop on. You the kind of nigger like to rip and run up and down the road in your car long 's you got a dime, but when you get broke and your belly get empty you run to your wife and cry on her shoulder. You just take one more step toward this door, and I bet you somebody'll be crying at your funeral. If you know anybody who care that much for you, you old yellow dog."

Daddy is quiet a while, and then I hear him crying. I don't feel good, because I don't like to hear Daddy and Mama crying. I look at Mama, but she's looking down in the fire.

"You never liked me," Daddy says.

"You said that before," Gran'mon says. "And I repeat, no, I never liked you, don't like you, and never will like you. Now, get out my yard 'fore I put the dog on you."

"I want see my boy," Daddy says, "I got a right to see my boy."

"In the first place, you ain't got no right in my yard," Gran'mon says.

"I want see my boy," Daddy says. "You might be able to keep me from seeing my wife, but you and nobody else can keep me from seeing my son. Half of him is me and I want see my—I want see him."

"You ain't leaving?" Gran'mon asks Daddy.

"I want see my boy," Daddy says. "And I'm go'n see my boy."

"Wait," Gran'mon says. "Your head hard. Wait till I come back. You go'n see all kind of boys."

Gran'mon comes back inside and goes to Uncle Al's room. I look toward the wall and I can hear Daddy moving on the gallery. I hear Mama crying and I look at her. I don't want see my mama crying, and I lay my head on Uncle Al's knee and I want cry, too.

"Amy, honey," Daddy calls, "ain't you coming up home and cook me something to eat? It's lonely up there without you, honey. You don't know how lonely it is without you. I can't stay up there without you, honey. Please come home. . . ."

I hear Gran'mon coming out of Uncle Al's room and I

look at her. Gran'mon's got Uncle Al's shotgun and she's putting a shell in it.

"Mama?" Mama screams.

"Don't worry," Gran'mon says. "I'm just go'n shoot over his head. I ain't go'n have them sending me to the pen for a good-for-nothing nigger like that."

"Mama, don't," Mama says. "He might hurt himself."

"Good," Gran'mon says. "Save me the trouble of doing it for him."

Mama runs to the wall. "Eddie, run," she screams. "Mama got the shotgun."

I hear Daddy going down the steps. I hear Spot running after him barking. Gran'mon knocks the door open with the gun barrel and shoot. I hear Daddy hollering.

"Mama, you didn't?" Mama says.

"I shot two miles over that nigger's head," Gran'mon says. "Long-legged coward."

We all run out on the gallery, and I see Daddy out in the road crying. I can see the people coming out on the galleries. They looking at us and they looking at Daddy. Daddy's standing out in the road crying.

"Boy, I would've like to seen old Eddie getting out of this yard," Uncle Al says.

Daddy's walking up and down the road in front of the house, and he's crying.

"Let's go back inside," Gran'mon says. "We won't be bothered with him for a while."

It's cold, and me and Uncle Al and Gran'mon go back inside. Mr. Freddie Jackson and Mama don't come back in right now, but after a little while they come in, too.

"Oh, Lord," Mama says.

Mama starts crying and Mr. Freddie Jackson takes her in his old arms. Mama lays her head on his old shoulder, but she just stays there a little while and then she moves.

"Can I go lay 'cross your bed, Uncle Al?" Mama asks.

"Sure," Uncle Al says.

I watch Mama going to Uncle Al's room.

"Well, I better be going," Mr. Freddie Jackson says.

"Freddie?" Gran'mon calls him, from the kitchen.

"Yes, ma'am?" he says.

"Come here a minute," Gran'mon says.

Mr. Freddie Jackson goes back in the kitchen where Gran'mon is. I get between Uncle Al's legs and look at the fire. Uncle Al rubs my head with his hand. Mr. Freddie Jackson comes out of the kitchen and goes in Uncle Al's room where Mama is. He must be sitting down on the bed because I can hear the springs.

"Gran'mon shot Daddy?" I ask.

Uncle Al rubs my head with his hand.

"She just scared him," he says. "You like your daddy?"

"Uh-huh."

"Your daddy's a good man," Uncle Al says. "A little foolish, but he's okay."

"I don't like Mr. Freddie Jackson," I say.

"How come?" Uncle Al says.

"I just don't like him," I say. "I just don't like him. I don't like him to hold my mama, neither. My daddy suppose to hold my mama. He ain't suppose to hold my mama."

"You want go back home?" Uncle Al asks.

"Uh-huh," I say. "But me and Mama go'n stay here now. I'm go'n sleep with you."

"But you rather go home and sleep in your own bed, huh?"

"Yes," I say. "I pull the cover 'way over my head. I like to sleep under the cover."

"You sleep like that all the time?" Uncle Al asks.

"Uh-huh."

"Even in the summertime, too?" Uncle Al says.

36

"Uh-huh," I say.

"Don't you ever get too warm?" Uncle Al says.

"Uh-uh," I say. "I feel good 'way under there."

Uncle Al rubs my head and I look down in the fire.

"Y'all come on in the kitchen and eat," Gran'mon calls.

Me and Uncle Al go back in the kitchen and sit down at the table. Gran'mon already got us food dished up. Uncle Al bows his head and I bow my head.

"Thank Thee, Father, for this food Thou has given us," Uncle Al says.

I raise my head and start eating. We having spaghetti for dinner. I pick up a string of spaghetti and suck it up in my mouth. I make it go *loo-loo-loo-loo-loo-loo-loop*. Uncle Al looks at me and laugh. I do it again, and Uncle Al laughs again.

"Don't play with my food," Gran'mon says. "Eat it right."

Gran'mon is standing 'side the stove looking at me. I don't like old Gran'mon. Shooting at my daddy—I don't like her.

"Taste good?" Uncle Al asks.

"Uh-huh," I say.

Uncle Al winks at me and wraps his spaghetti on his fork and sticks it in his mouth. I try to wrap mine on my fork, but it keeps falling off. I can just pick up one at a time.

Gran'mon starts singing her song again. She fools round the stove a little while, and then she goes in the front room. I get a string of spaghetti and suck it up in my mouth. When I hear her coming back I stop and eat right.

"Still out there," she says. "Sitting on that ditch bank crying like a baby. Let him cry. But he better not come back in this yard."

Gran'mon goes over to the stove and sticks a piece of wood in the fire. She starts singing again:

Oh, I'll be there,
I'll be there,
When the roll is called in Heaven, I'll be there.

Uncle Al finishes his dinner and waits for me. When I finish eating, me and him go in the front room and sit at the fire.

"I want go to the toilet, Uncle Al," I say.

I get my coat and cap and bring them to the fireplace, and Uncle Al helps me get in them. Uncle Al buttons up my coat for me, and I go out on the gallery. I look out in the road and I see Daddy sitting out on the ditch bank. I go round the house and go back to the toilet. The grass is dry like hay. There ain't no leaves on the trees. I see some birds in the tree. The wind's moving the birds's feathers. I bet you them little birds's some cold. I'm glad I'm not a bird. No daddy, no mama—I'm glad I'm not a bird.

I open the door and go in the toilet. I get up on the seat and pull down my pants. I squat over the hole—but I better not slip and fall in there. I'll get all that poo-poo on my feet, and Gran'mon'll kill me if I tramp all that poo-poo in her house.

I try hard and my poo-poo come. It's long. I like to poo-poo. Sometimes I poo-poo on my pot at night. Mama don't like for me to go back to the toilet when it's late. Scared a snake might bite me.

I finish poo-poo-ing and I jump down from the seat and pull up my pants. I look in the hole and I see my poo-poo. I look in the top of the toilet, but I don't see any spiders. We got spiders in us toilet. Gran'mon must be done killed all her spiders with some Flit.

I push the door open and I go back to the front of the house. I go round the gallery and I see Daddy standing at the gate looking in the yard. He sees me.

"Sonny?" he calls.

"Hanh?"

"Come here, baby," he says.

I look toward the door, but I don't see nobody and I go to the gate where Daddy is. Daddy pushes the gate open and grabs me and hugs me to him.

"You still love your daddy, Sonny?" he asks.

"Uh-huh," I say.

Daddy hugs me and kisses me on the face.

"I love my baby," he says. "I love my baby. Where your mama?"

"Laying 'cross Uncle Al's bed in his room," I say. "And Mr. Freddie Jackson in there, too."

Daddy pushes me away real quickly and looks in my face.

"Who else in there?" he asks. "Who?"

"Just them," I say. "Uncle Al's in Gran'mon's room by the fire, and Gran'mon's in the kitchen."

Daddy looks toward the house.

"This the last straw," he says. "I'm turning your Gran'-mon in this minute. And you go'n be my witness. Come on."

"Where we going?" I ask.

"To that preacher's house," Daddy says. "And if he can't help me, I'm going back in the field to Madame Toussaint."

Daddy grabs my hand and me and him go up the quarter. I can see all the children going back to school.

". . . Lock her own daughter in a room with another man and got her little grandson there looking all the time," Daddy says. "She ain't so much Christian as she put out to be. Singing round that house every time you bat your eyes and doing something like that in broad daylight. Step it up, Sonny."

"I'm coming fast as I can," I say.

"I'll see about that," Daddy says. "I'll see about that."

When me and Daddy get to Reverend Simmons's house, we go up on the gallery and Daddy knocks on the door. Mrs. Carey comes to the door to see what we want.

"Mrs. Carey, is the Reverend in?" Daddy asks.

"Yes," Mrs. Carey says. "Come on in."

Me and Daddy go inside and I see Reverend Simmons sitting at the fireplace. Reverend Simmons got on his eyeglasses and he's reading the Bible. He turns and looks at us when we come in. He takes off his glasses like he can't see us too good with them on, and he looks at us again. Mrs. Carey goes back in the kitchen and me and Daddy go over to the fireplace.

"Good evening, Reverend," Daddy says.

"Good evening," Reverend Simmons says. "Hi, Sonny."

"Hi," I say.

"Reverend, I hate busting in on you like this, but I need your help," Daddy says. "Reverend, Amy done left me and her mama got her down at her house with another man and—"

"Now, calm down a second," Reverend Simmons says. He looks toward the kitchen. "Carey, bring Mr. Howard and Sonny a chair."

Mrs. Carey brings the chairs and goes right on back in the kitchen again. Daddy turns his chair so he can be facing Reverend Simmons.

"I come in pretty late last night 'cause my car broke down on me and I had to walk all the way—from the other side of Morgan up there," Daddy says. "When I get home me and Amy get in a little squabble. This morning we squabble again, but I don't think too much of it. You know a man and a woman go'n have their little squabbles every once in a while. I go to work in the field. Work like a dog. Cutting cane right and left—trying to make up lost time I spent at the house this morning. When I come home for dinner—hungry 's a dog—my wife, neither my boy is there. No dinner—and I'm hungry 's a dog. I go in the front room and all their clothes gone. Lord, I almost go crazy. I don't know what to do. I run out the house because I think she still mad at me and done gone down to her mama. I go down there and ask for her, and first thing I know here come Mama Rachel shooting at me with Uncle Al's shotgun."

"I can't believe that," Reverend Simmons says.

"If I'm telling a lie I hope to never rise from this chair," Daddy says. "And I reckon she would've got me if I wasn't moving fast."

"That don't sound like Sister Rachel," Reverend Simmons says.

"Sound like her or don't sound like her, she did it," Daddy says. "Sonny right over there. He seen every bit of it. Ask him."

Reverend Simmons looks at me but he don't ask me nothing. He just clicks his tongue and shakes his head.

"That don't sound like Sister Rachel," he says. "But if you say that's what she did, I'll go down there and talk to her."

"And that ain't all," Daddy says.

Reverend Simmons waits for Daddy to go on.

"She got Freddie Jackson locked up in a room with Amy," Daddy says.

Reverend Simmons looks at me and Daddy, then he goes over and gets his coat and hat from against the wall. Reverend Simmons's coat is long and black. His hat is big like a cowboy's hat.

"I'll be down the quarter, Carey," he tells Mrs. Simmons. "Be back quick as I can."

We go out of the house and Daddy holds my hand. Me and him and Reverend Simmons go out in the road and head on back down the quarter.

"Reverend Simmons, I want my wife back," Daddy says. "A man can't live by himself in this world. It too cold and cruel."

Reverend Simmons don't say nothing to Daddy. He starts humming a little song to himself. Reverend Simmons is big and he can walk fast. He takes big old long steps and me and Daddy got to walk fast to keep up with him. I got to run because Daddy's got my hand.

We get to Gran'mon's house and Reverend Simmons pushes the gate open and goes in the yard.

"Me and Sonny'll stay out here," Daddy says.

"I'm cold, Daddy," I say.

"I'll build a fire," Daddy says. "You want me build me and you a little fire?"

"Uh-huh."

"Help me get some sticks, then," Daddy says.

Me and Daddy get some grass and weeds and Daddy finds a big chunk of dry wood. We pile it all up and Daddy gets a match out his pocket and lights the fire.

"Feel better?" he says.

"Uh-huh."

"How come you not in school this evening?" Daddy asks.

"I wee-weed on myself," I say.

I tell Daddy because I know Daddy ain't go'n whip me.

"You peed on yourself at school?" Daddy asks. "Sonny, I thought you was a big boy. That's something little babies do."

"Miss Hebert want see you and Mama," I say.

"I don't have time to see nobody now," Daddy says. "I got my own troubles. I just hope that preacher in there can do something."

I look up at Daddy, but he's looking down in the fire.

"Sonny?" I hear Mama calling me.

I turn and I see Mama and all of them standing out there on the gallery.

"Hanh?" I answer.

"Come in here before you catch a death of cold," Mama says.

Daddy goes to the fence and looks across the pickets at Mama.

"Amy," he says, "please come home. I swear I ain't go'n do it no more."

"Sonny, you hear me talking to you?" Mama calls.

"I ain't go'n catch cold," I say. "We got a fire. I'm warm."

"Amy, please come home," Daddy says. "Please, honey. I forgive you. I forgive Mama. I forgive everybody. Just come home."

I look at Mama and Reverend Simmons talking on the gallery. The others ain't talking; they just standing there looking out in the road at me and Daddy. Reverend Simmons comes out the yard and over to the fire. Daddy comes to the fire where me and Reverend Simmons is. He looks at Reverend Simmons but Reverend Simmons won't look back at him.

"Well, Reverend?" Daddy says.

"She say she tired of you and that car," Reverend Simmons says.

Daddy falls down on the ground and cries.

"A man just can't live by himself in this cold, cruel world," he says. "He got to have a woman to stand by him. He just can't make it by himself. God, help me."

"Be strong, man," Reverend Simmons says.

"I can't be strong with my wife in there and me out here," Daddy says. "I need my wife."

"Well, you go'n have to straighten that out the best way you can," Reverend Simmons says. "And I talked to Sister Rachel. She said she didn't shoot to hurt you. She just shot to kind of scare you away."

"She didn't shoot to hurt me?" Daddy says. "And I reckon

them things was jelly beans I heard zooming just three inches over my head?"

"She said she didn't shoot to hurt you," Reverend Simmons says. He holds his hands over the fire. "This fire's good, but I got to get on back up the quarter. Got to get my wood for tonight. I'll see you people later. And I hope everything comes out all right."

"Reverend, you sure you can't do nothing?" Daddy asks.

"I tried, son," Reverend Simmons says. "Now we'll leave it in God's hand."

"But I want my wife back now," Daddy says. "God take so long to—"

"Mr. Howard, that's blasphemous," Reverend Simmons says.

"I don't want blaspheme Him," Daddy says. "But I'm in a mess. I'm in a big mess. I want my wife."

"I'd suggest you kneel down sometime," Reverend Simmons says. "That always helps in a family."

Reverend Simmons looks at me like he's feeling sorry for me, then he goes on back up the quarter. I can see his coattail hitting him round the knees.

"You coming in this yard, Sonny?" Mama calls.

"I'm with Daddy," I say.

Mama goes back in the house and Gran'mon and them follow her.

"When you want one of them preachers to do something for you, they can't do a doggone thing," Daddy says. "Nothing but stand up in that churchhouse and preach 'bout Heaven. I hate to go to that old hoo-doo woman, but I reckon there ain't nothing else I can do. You want go back there with me, Sonny?"

"Uh-huh."

"Come on," Daddy says.

Daddy takes my hand and me and him leave the fire.

When I get 'way down the quarter I look back and see the fire still burning. We cross the railroad tracks and I can see the people cutting cane. They got plenty cane all on the ground.

"Get me piece of cane, Daddy," I say.

"Sonny, please," Daddy says. "I'm thinking."

"I want piece of two-ninety," I say.

Daddy turns my hand loose and jumps over the ditch. He finds a piece of two-ninety and jumps back over. Daddy takes out a little pocketknife and peels the cane. He gives me a round and he cut him off a round and chew it. I like two-ninety cane because it's soft and sweet and got plenty juice in it.

"I want another piece," I say.

Daddy cuts me off another round and hands it to me.

"I'll be glad when you big enough to peel your own cane," he says.

"I can peel my own cane now," I say.

Daddy breaks me off three joints and hands it to me. I peel the cane with my teeth. Two-ninety cane is soft and it's easy to peel.

Me and Daddy go round the bend, and then I can see Madame Toussaint's house. Madame Toussaint's got a' old house, and look like it want to fall down any minute. I'm scared of Madame Toussaint. Billy Joe Martin say Madame Toussaint's a witch, and he say one time he seen Madame Toussaint riding a broom.

Daddy pulls Madame Toussaint's little old broken-down gate open and we go in the yard. Me and Daddy go far as the steps, but we don't go up on the gallery. Madame Toussaint's got plenty trees round her house, little trees and big trees. And she got plenty moss hanging on every tree. I see a pecan over there on the ground but I'm scared to go and pick it up. Madame Toussaint'll put bad mark on me and I'll turn to a frog or something. I let Madame Toussaint's little old pecan stay right where it is. And I go up to Daddy and let him hold my hand.

"Madame Toussaint?" Daddy calls.

Madame Toussaint don't answer. Like she ain't there.

"Madame Toussaint?" Daddy calls again.

"Who that?" Madame Toussaint answers.

"Me," Daddy says. "Eddie Howard and his little boy Sonny."

"What you want, Eddie Howard?" Madame Toussaint calls from in her house.

"I want talk to you," Daddy says. "I need little advice on something."

I hear a dog bark three times in the house. He must be a big old dog because he's sure got a heavy voice. Madame Toussaint comes to the door and cracks it open.

"Can I come in?" Daddy says.

"Come in, Eddie Howard," Madame Toussaint says.

Me and Daddy go up the steps and Madame Toussaint opens the door for us. Madame Toussaint's a little bitty little old woman and her face is brown like cowhide. I look at Madame Toussaint and I walk close 'side Daddy. Me and Daddy go in the house and Madame Toussaint shuts the door and comes back to her fireplace. She sits down in her big old rocking chair and looks at me and Daddy. I look round Daddy's leg at Madame Toussaint, but I let Daddy hold my hand. Madame Toussaint's house don't smell good. It's too dark in here. It don't smell good at all. Madame Toussaint ought to have a window or something open in her house.

"I need some advice, Madame Toussaint," Daddy says.

"Your wife left you," Madame Toussaint says.

"How you know?" Daddy asks.

"That's all you men come back here for," Madame Toussaint says. "That's how I know."

Daddy nods his head. "Yes," he says. "She done left me and staying with another man."

"She left," Madame Toussaint says. "But she's not staying with another man."

"Yes, she is," Daddy says.

"She's not," Madame Toussaint says. "You trying to tell me my business?"

"No, ma'am," Daddy says.

"I should hope not," Madame Toussaint says.

Madame Toussaint ain't got but three old rotten teeth in her mouth. I bet you she can't peel no cane with them old rotten teeth. I bet you they'd break off in a hard piece of cane.

"I need advice, Madame Toussaint," Daddy says.

"You got money?" Madame Toussaint asks.

"I got some," Daddy says.

"How much?" she asks Daddy. She's looking up at Daddy like she don't believe him.

Daddy turns my hand loose and sticks his hand down in his pocket. He gets all his money out his pocket and leans over the fire to see how much he's got. I see some matches and piece of string and some nails in Daddy's hand. I reach for the piece of string and Daddy taps me on the hand with his other hand.

"I got about seventy-five cents," Daddy says. "Counting them pennies."

"My price is three dollars," Madame Toussaint says.

"I can cut you a load of wood," Daddy says. "Or make grocery for you. I'll do anything in the world if you can help me, Madame Toussaint."

"Three dollars," Madame Toussaint says. "I got all the wood I'll need this winter. Enough grocery to last me till summer."

"But this all I got," Daddy says.

"When you get more, come back," Madame Toussaint says.

"But I want my wife back now," Daddy says. "I can't wait till I get more money."

"Three dollars is my price," Madame Toussaint says. "No more, no less."

"But can't you give me just a little advice for seventy-five cents?" Daddy says. "Seventy-five cents worth? Maybe I can start from there and figure something out."

Madame Toussaint looks at me and looks at Daddy again.

"You say that's your boy?" she says.

"Yes, ma'am," Daddy says.

"Nice-looking boy," Madame Toussaint says.

"His name's Sonny," Daddy says.

"Hi, Sonny," Madame Toussaint says.

"Say 'Hi' to Madame Toussaint," Daddy says. "Go on."

"Hi," I say, sticking close to Daddy.

"Well, Madame Toussaint?" Daddy says.

"Give me the money," Madame Toussaint says. "Don't complain to me if you not satisfied."

"Don't worry," Daddy says. "I won't complain. Anything to get her back home."

Daddy leans over the fire again and picks the money out of his hand. Then he reaches it to Madame Toussaint.

"Give me that little piece of string," Madame Toussaint says. "It might come in handy sometime in the future. Wait," she says. "Run it 'cross the left side of the boy's face three times, then pass it to me behind your back."

"What's that for?" Daddy asks.

"Just do like I say," Madame Toussaint says.

"Yes, ma'am," Daddy says. Daddy turns to me. "Hold still, Sonny," he says. He rubs the little old dirty piece of cord over my face, and then he sticks his hand behind his back.

Madame Toussaint reaches in her pocket and takes out her pocketbook. She opens it and puts the money in. She opens another little compartment and stuffs the string down in it. Then she snaps the pocketbook and puts it back in her pocket. She picks up three little green sticks she got tied together and starts poking in the fire with them.

"What's the advice?" Daddy asks.

Madame Toussaint don't say nothing.

"Madame Toussaint?" Daddy says.

Madame Toussaint still don't answer him, she just looks down in the fire. Her face is red from the fire. I get scared of Madame Toussaint. She can ride all over the plantation on her broom. Billy Joe Martin say he seen her one night riding 'cross the houses. She was whipping her broom with three switches.

Madame Toussaint raises her head and looks at Daddy. Her eyes's big and white, and I get scared of her. I hide my face 'side Daddy's leg.

"Give it up," I hear her say.

"Give what up?" Daddy says.

"Give it up," she says.

"What?" Daddy says.

"Give it up," she says.

"I don't even know what you talking 'bout," Daddy says. "How can I give up something and I don't even know what it is?"

"I said it three times," Madame Toussaint says. "No more, no less. Up to you now to follow it through from there."

"Follow what from where?" Daddy says. "You said three little old words: 'Give it up.' I don't know no more now than I knowed 'fore I got here."

"I told you you wasn't go'n be satisfied," Madame Toussaint says.

"Satisfied?" Daddy says. "Satisfied for what? You gived me just three little old words and you want me to be satisfied?"

"You can leave," Madame Toussaint says.

"Leave?" Daddy says. "You mean I give you seventy-five cents for three words? A quarter a word? And I'm leaving? No, Lord."

"Rollo?" Madame Toussaint says.

I see Madame Toussaint's big old black dog get up out of the corner and come where she is. Madame Toussaint pats the dog on the head with her hand.

"Two dollars and twenty-five cents more and you get all the advice you need," Madame Toussaint says.

"Can't I get you a load of wood and fix your house for you or something?" Daddy says.

"I don't want my house fixed and I don't need no more wood," Madame Toussaint says. "I got three loads of wood just three days ago from a man who didn't have money. Before I know it I'll have wood piled up all over my yard."

"Can't I do anything?" Daddy says.

"You can leave," Madame Toussaint says. "I ought to have somebody else dropping round pretty soon. Lately I've been having men dropping in three times a day. All of them just like you. What they can do to make their wives love them more. What they can do to keep their wives from running round with some other man. What they can do to make their wives give in. What they can do to make their wives scratch their backs. What they can do to make their wives look at them when they talking to her. Get out my house before I put the dog on you. You been here too long for seventy-five cents."

Madame Toussaint's big old jet-black dog gives three loud barks that makes my head hurt. Madame Toussaint pats him on the back to calm him down.

"Come on, Sonny," Daddy says.

I let Daddy take my hand and we go over to the door.

"I still don't feel like you helped me very much, though," Daddy says.

Madame Toussaint pats her big old jet-black dog on the

head and she don't answer Daddy. Daddy pushes the door open and we go outside. It's some cold outside. Me and Daddy go down Madame Toussaint's old broken-down steps.

"What was them words?" Daddy asks me.

"Hanh?"

"What she said when she looked up out of that fire?" Daddy asks.

"I was scared," I say. "Her face was red and her eyes got big and white. I was scared. I had to hide my face."

"Didn't you hear what she told me?" Daddy asks.

"She told you three dollars," I say.

"I mean when she looked up," Daddy says.

"She say, 'Give it up,' " I say.

"Yes," Daddy says. " 'Give it up.' Give what up? I don't even know what she's talking 'bout. I hope she don't mean give you and Amy up. She ain't that crazy. I don't know nothing else she can be talking 'bout. You don't know, do you?"

"Uh-uh," I say.

" 'Give it up,' " Daddy says. "I don't even know what she's talking 'bout. I wonder who them other men was she was speaking of. Johnny and his wife had a fight the other week. It might be him. Frank Armstrong and his wife had a round couple weeks back. Could be him. I wish I knowed what she told them."

"I want another piece of cane," I say.

"No," Daddy says. "You'll be pee-ing in bed all night tonight."

"I'm go'n sleep with Uncle Al," I say. "Me and him go'n sleep in his bed."

"Please, be quiet, Sonny," Daddy says. "I got enough troubles on my mind. Don't add more to it."

Me and Daddy walk in the middle of the road. Daddy holds my hand. I can hear a tractor—I see it across the field. The people loading cane on the trailer back of the tractor.

"Come on," Daddy says. "We going over to Frank Armstrong."

Daddy totes me 'cross the ditch on his back. I ride on Daddy's back and I look at the stubbles where the people done cut the cane. Them rows some long. Plenty cane's laying on the ground. I can see cane all over the field. Me and Daddy go over where the people cutting cane.

"How come you ain't working this evening?" a man asks Daddy. The man's shucking a big armful of cane with his cane knife.

"Frank Armstrong round anywhere?" Daddy asks the man.

"Farther over," the man says. "Hi, youngster."

"Hi," I say.

Me and Daddy go 'cross the field. I look at the people cutting cane. That cane is some tall. I want another piece, but I might wee-wee in Uncle Al's bed.

Me and Daddy go over where Mr. Frank Armstrong and Mrs. Julie's cutting cane. Mrs. Julie got overalls on just like Mr. Frank got. She's even wearing one of Mr. Frank's old hats.

"How y'all?" Daddy says.

"So-so, and yourself?" Mrs. Julie says.

"I'm trying to make it," Daddy says. "Can I borrow your husband there a minute?"

"Sure," Mrs. Julie says. "But don't keep him too long. We trying to reach the end 'fore dark."

"It won't take long," Daddy says.

Mr. Frank and them got a little fire burning in one of the middles. Me and him and Daddy go over there. Daddy squats down and let me slide off his back.

"What's the trouble?" Mr. Frank asks Daddy.

"Amy left me, Frank," Daddy says.

Mr. Frank holds his hands over the fire.

"She left you?" he says.

"Yes," Daddy says. "And I want her back, Frank."

"What can I do?" Mr. Frank says. "She's no kin to me. I can't go and make her come back."

"I thought maybe you could tell me what you and Madame Toussaint talked about," Daddy says. "That's if you don't mind, Frank."

"What?" Mr. Frank says. "Who told you I talked with Madame Toussaint?"

"Nobody," Daddy says. "But I heard you and Julie had a fight, and I thought maybe you went back to her for advice."

"For what?" Mr. Frank says.

"So you and Julie could make up," Daddy says.

"Well, I'll be damned," Mr. Frank says. "I done heard everything. Excuse me, Sonny. But your daddy's enough to make anybody cuss."

I look up at Daddy, and I look back in the fire again.

"Please, Frank," Daddy says. "I'm desperate. I'm ready to try anything. I'll do anything to get her back in my house."

"Why don't you just go and get her?" Mr. Frank says. "That makes sense."

"I can't," Daddy says. "Mama won't let me come in the yard. She even took a shot at me once today."

"What?" Mr. Frank says. He looks at Daddy, and then he just bust out laughing. Daddy laughs little bit, too.

"What y'all talked about, Frank?" Daddy asks. "Maybe if I try the same thing, maybe I'll be able to get her back, too."

Mr. Frank laughs at Daddy, then he stops and just looks at Daddy.

"No," he says. "I'm afraid my advice won't help your case. You got to first get close to your wife. And your mother-in-law won't let you do that. No, mine won't help you."

"It might," Daddy says.

53

"No, it won't," Mr. Frank says.

"It might," Daddy says. "What was it?"

"All right," Mr. Frank says. "She told me I wasn't petting Julie enough."

"Petting her?" Daddy says.

"You think he knows what we talking 'bout?" Mr. Frank asks Daddy.

"I'll get him piece of cane," Daddy says.

They got a big pile of cane right behind Daddy's back, and he crosses the row and gets me a stalk of two-ninety. He breaks off three joints and hands it to me. He throws the rest of the stalk back.

"So I start petting her," Mr. Frank says.

"What you mean 'petting her'?" Daddy says. "I don't even know what you mean now."

"Eddie, I swear," Mr. Frank says. "Stroking her. You know. Like you stroke a colt. A little horse."

"Oh," Daddy says. "Did it work?"

"What you think?" Mr. Frank says, grinning. "Every night, a little bit. Turn your head, Sonny."

"Hanh?"

"Look the other way," Daddy says.

I look down the row toward the other end. I don't see nothing but cane all over the ground.

"Stroke her a little back here," Mr. Frank says. I hear him hitting on his pants. "Works every time. Get along now like two peas in one pod. Every night when we get in the bed—" I hear him hitting again. "—couple little strokes. Now everything's all right."

"You was right," Daddy says. "That won't help me none."

"My face getting cold," I say.

"You can turn round and warm," Daddy says.

I turn and look at Mr. Frank. I bite off piece of cane and chew it.

"I told you it wouldn't," Mr. Frank says. "Well, I got to get back to work. What you go'n do now?"

"I don't know," Daddy says. "If I had three dollars she'd give me some advice. But I don't have a red copper. You wouldn't have three dollars you could spare till payday, huh?"

"I don't have a dime," Mr. Frank says. "Since we made up, Julie keeps most of the money."

"You think she'd lend me three dollars till Saturday?" Daddy asks.

"I don't know if she got that much on her," Mr. Frank says. "I'll go over and ask her."

I watch Mr. Frank going 'cross the rows where Mrs. Julie's cutting cane. They start talking, and then I hear them laughing.

"You warm?" Daddy asks.

"Uh-huh."

I see Mr. Frank coming back to the fire.

"She don't have it on her but she got it at the house," Mr. Frank says. "If you can wait till we knock off."

"No," Daddy says. "I can't wait till night. I got to try to borrow it from somebody now."

"Why don't you go 'cross the field and try Johnny Green," Mr. Frank says. "He's always got some money. Maybe he'll lend it to you."

"I'll ask him," Daddy says. "Get on, Sonny."

Me and Daddy go back 'cross the field. I can hear Mr. Johnny Green singing, and Daddy turns that way and we go down where Mr. Johnny is. Mr. Johnny stops his singing when he sees me and Daddy. He chops the top off a' armful of cane and throws it 'cross the row. Mr. Johnny's cutting cane all by himself.

"Hi, Brother Howard," Mr. Johnny says.

"Hi," Daddy says. Daddy squats down and let me slide off.

"Hi there, little Brother Sonny," Mr. Johnny says.

"Hi," I say.

"How you?" Mr. Johnny asks.

"I'm all right," I say.

"That's good," Mr. Johnny says. "And how you this beautiful, God-sent day, Brother Howard?"

"I'm fine," Daddy says. "Johnny, I want know if you can spare me 'bout three dollars till Saturday?"

"Sure, Brother Howard," Mr. Johnny says. "You mind telling me just why you need it? I don't mind lending a good brother anything, long 's I know he ain't wasting it on women or drink."

"I want pay Madame Toussaint for some advice," Daddy says.

"Little trouble, Brother?" Mr. Johnny asks.

"Amy done left me, Johnny," Daddy says. "I need some advice. I just got to get her back."

"I know what you mean, Brother," Mr. Johnny says. "I had to visit Madame—you won't carry this no farther, huh?"

"No," Daddy says.

"Couple months ago I had to take a little trip back there to see her," Mr. Johnny says.

"What was wrong?" Daddy asks.

"Little misunderstanding between me and Sister Laura," Mr. Johnny says.

"She helped?" Daddy asks.

"Told me to stop spending so much time in church and little more time at home," Mr. Johnny says. "I couldn't see that. You know, far back as I can go in my family my people been good church members."

"I know that," Daddy says.

"My pappy was a deacon and my mammy didn't miss a

56

Sunday long as I can remember," Mr. Johnny says. "And that's how I was raised. To fear God. I just couldn't see it when she first told me that. But I thought it over. I went for a long walk back in the field. I got down on my knees and looked up at the sky. I asked God to show me the way—to tell me what to do. And He did, He surely did. He told me to do just like Madame Toussaint said. Slack up going to church. Go twice a week, but spend the rest of the time with her. Just like that He told me. And I'm doing exactly what He said. Twice a week. And, Brother Howard, don't spread this round, but the way Sister Laura been acting here lately, there might be a little Johnny next summer sometime."

"No?" Daddy says.

"Uhnnnn-hunh," Mr. Johnny says.

"I'll be doggone," Daddy says. "I'm glad to hear that."

"I'll be the happiest man on this whole plantation," Mr. Johnny says.

"I know how you feel," Daddy says. "Yes, I know how you feel. But that three, can you lend it to me?"

"Sure, Brother," Mr. Johnny says. "Anything to bring a family back together. Nothing more important in this world than family love. Yes, indeed."

Mr. Johnny unbuttons his top overalls pocket and takes out a dollar.

"Only thing I got is five, Brother Howard," he says. "You wouldn't happen to have some change, would you?"

"I don't have a red copper," Daddy says. "But I'll be more than happy if you can let me have that five. I need some grocery in the house, too."

"Sure, Brother," Mr. Johnny says. He hands Daddy the dollar. "Nothing looks more beautiful than a family at a table eating something the little woman just cooked. But you did say Saturday didn't you, Brother?"

"Yes," Daddy says. "I'll pay you back soon 's I get paid. You can't ever guess how much this means to me, Johnny."

"Glad I can help, Brother," Mr. Johnny says. "Hope she can do likewise."

"I hope so too," Daddy says. "Anyhow, this a start."

"See you Saturday, Brother," Mr. Johnny says.

"Soon 's I get paid," Daddy says. "Hop on, Sonny, and hold tight. We going back."

4: Daddy walks up on Madame Toussaint's gallery and knocks on the door.

"Who that?" Madame Toussaint asks.

"Me. Eddie Howard," Daddy says. He squats down so I can slide off his back. I slide down and let Daddy hold my hand.

"What you want, Eddie Howard?" Madame Toussaint asks.

"I got three dollars," Daddy says. "I still want that advice."

Madame Toussaint's big old jet-black dog barks three times, and then I hear Madame Toussaint coming to the door. She peeps through the keyhole at me and Daddy. She opens the door and let me and Daddy come in. We go to the fireplace and warm. Madame Toussaint comes to the fireplace and sits down in her big old rocking chair. She looks up at Daddy. I look for big old Rollo, but I don't see him. He must be under the bed or hiding somewhere in the corner.

"You got three dollars?" Madame Toussaint asks Daddy.

"Yes," Daddy says. He takes out the dollar and shows it to Madame Toussaint.

Madame Toussaint holds her hand up for it.

"This is five," Daddy says. "I want two back."

"You go'n get your two," Madame Toussaint says.

"Come to think of it," Daddy says, "I ought to just owe you two and a quarter, since I done already gived you seventy-five cents."

"You want advice?" Madame Toussaint asks Daddy. Madame Toussaint looks like she's getting mad with Daddy now.

"Sure," Daddy says. "But since—"

"Then shut up and hand me your money," Madame Toussaint says.

"But I done already—" Daddy says.

"Get out my house, nigger," Madame Toussaint says. "And don't come back till you learn how to act."

"All right," Daddy says, "I'll give you three more dollars."

He hands Madame Toussaint the dollar.

Madame Toussaint gets her pocketbook out her pocket. Then she leans close to the fire so she can look down in it. She sticks her hand in the pocketbook and gets two dollars. She looks at the two dollars a long time. She stands up and gets her eyeglasses off the mantelpiece and puts them on her eyes. She looks at the two dollars a long time, then she hands them to Daddy. She sticks the dollar bill Daddy gived her in the pocketbook, then she takes her eyeglasses off and puts them back on the mantelpiece. Madame Toussaint sits in her big old rocking chair and starts poking in the fire with the three sticks again. Her face gets red from the fire, her eyes get big and white. I turn my head and hide behind Daddy's leg.

"Go set fire to your car," Madame Toussaint says.

"What?" Daddy says.

"Go set fire to your car," Madame Toussaint says.

"You talking to me?" Daddy says.

"Go set fire to your car," Madame Toussaint says.

"Now, just a minute," Daddy says. "I didn't give you my hard-earned three dollars for that kind of foolishness. I dismiss that seventy-five cents you took from me, but not my three dollars that easy."

"You want your wife back?" Madame Toussaint asks Daddy.

"That's what I'm paying you for," Daddy says.

"Then go set fire to your car," Madame Toussaint says. "You can't have both."

"You must be fooling," Daddy says.

"I don't fool," Madame Toussaint says. "You paid for advice and I'm giving you advice."

"You mean that?" Daddy says. "You mean I got to go burn up my car for Amy to come back home?"

"If you want her back there," Madame Toussaint says. "Do you?"

"I wouldn't be standing here if I didn't," Daddy says.

"Then go and burn it up," Madame Toussaint says. "A gallon of coal oil and a penny box of match ought to do the trick. You got any gas in it?"

"A little bit—if nobody ain't drained it," Daddy says.

"Then you can use that," Madame Toussaint says. "But if you want her back there you got to burn it up. That's my advice to you. And if I was you I'd do it right away. You can never tell."

"Tell about what?" Daddy asks.

"She might be sleeping in another man's bed a week from now," Madame Toussaint says. "This man loves her and he's kind. And that's what a woman wants. That's what they need. You men don't know this, but you better learn it before it's too late."

"What's that other man's name?" Daddy asks. "Can it be Freddie Jackson?"

"It can," Madame Toussaint says. "But it don't have to be. Any man that'd give her love and kindness."

"I love her," Daddy says. "I give her kindness. I'm always giving her love and kindness."

"When you home, you mean," Madame Toussaint says. "How about when you running up and down the road in your car? How do you think she feels then?"

Daddy don't say nothing.

"You men better learn," Madame Toussaint says. "Now, if you want her, go and burn it. If you don't want her, go and get drunk off them two dollars and sleep in a cold bed tonight."

"You mean she'll come back tonight?" Daddy asks.

"She's ready to come back right now," Madame Toussaint says. "Poor little thing."

I look round Daddy's leg at Madame Toussaint. Madame Toussaint's looking in the fire. Her face ain't red no more; her eyes ain't big and white, either.

"She's not happy where she is," Madame Toussaint says.

"She's with her mama," Daddy says.

"You don't have to tell me my business," Madame Toussaint says. "I know where she is. And I still say she's not happy. She much rather be back in her own house. Women like to be in their own house. That's their world. You men done messed up the outside world so bad that they feel lost and out of place in it. Her house is her world. Only there she can do what she want. She can't do that in anybody else house—mama or nobody else. But you men don't know any of this. Y'all never know how a woman feels, because you never ask how she feels. Long 's she there when you get there you satisfied. Long 's you give her two or three dollars every weekend you think she ought to be satisfied. But keep on. One day all of you'll find out."

"Couldn't I sell the car or something?" Daddy asks.

"You got to burn it," Madame Toussaint says. "How come your head so hard?"

"But I paid good money for that car," Daddy says. "It wouldn't look right if I just jumped up and put fire to it."

"You, get out my house," Madame Toussaint says, pointing her finger at Daddy. "Go do what you want with your car. It's yours. But just don't come back here bothering me for no more advice."

"I don't know," Daddy says.

"I'm through talking," Madame Toussaint says. "Rollo? Come here, baby."

Big old jet-black Rollo comes up and puts his head in Madame Toussaint's lap. Madame Toussaint pats him on the head.

"That's what I got to do, hanh?" Daddy says.

Madame Toussaint don't answer Daddy. She starts singing a song to Rollo:

> Mama's little baby,
> Mama's little baby.

"He bad?" Daddy asks.

> Mama's little baby,
> Mama's little baby.

"Do he bite?" Daddy asks.

Madame Toussaint keeps on singing:

> Mama's little baby,
> Mama's little baby.

"Come on," Daddy says. "I reckon we better be going."

Daddy squats down and I climb up on his back. I look down at Madame Toussaint patting big old jet-black Rollo on his head.

Daddy pushes the door open and we go outside. It's cold outside. Daddy goes down Madame Toussaint's three old broken-down steps and we go out in the road.

"I don't know," Daddy says.

"Hanh?"

"I'm talking to myself," Daddy says. "I don't know about burning up my car."

"You go'n burn up your car?" I ask.

"That's what Madame Toussaint say to do," Daddy says.

"You ain't go'n have no more car?"

"I reckon not," Daddy says. "You want me and Mama to stay together?"

"Uh-huh."

"Then I reckon I got to burn it up," Daddy says. "But I sure hope there was another way out. I put better than three hundred dollars in that car."

Daddy walks fast and I bounce on his back.

"God, I wish there was another way out," Daddy says. "Don't look like that's right for a man to just jump up and set fire to something like that. What you think I ought to do?"

"Hanh?"

"Go back to sleep," Daddy says. "I don't know what I'm educating you for."

"I ain't sleeping," I say.

"I don't know," Daddy says. "That don't look right. All Frank Armstrong had to do was pop Julie on the butt little bit every night 'fore she went to sleep. All Johnny had to do was stop going to church so much. Neither one of them had to burn down anything. Johnny didn't have to burn down the church; Frank didn't have to burn down the bed— nothing. But me, I got to burn up my car. She charged all us the same thing—no, she even charged me seventy-five cents more, and I got to burn up a car I can still get some use out. Now, that don't sound right, do it?"

"Hanh?"

"I can't figure it," Daddy says. "Look like I ought to be able to sell it for little something. Get some of my money back. Burning it, I don't get a red copper. That just don't sound right to me. I wonder if she was fooling. No. She say she wasn't. But maybe that wasn't my advice she seen in that fireplace. Maybe that was somebody else advice. Maybe she gived me the wrong one. Maybe it belongs to the man coming back there after me. They go there three times a day, she can get them mixed up."

"I'm scared of Madame Toussaint, Daddy," I say.

"Must've been somebody else," Daddy says. "I bet it was. I bet you anything it was."

I bounce on Daddy's back and I close my eyes. I open them and I see me and Daddy going 'cross the railroad tracks. We go up the quarter to Gran'mon's house. Daddy squats down and I slide off his back.

"Run in the house to the fire," Daddy says. "Tell your mama come to the door."

Soon 's I come in the yard, Spot runs down the walk and starts barking. Mama and all of them come out on the gallery.

"My baby," Mama says. Mama comes down the steps and hugs me to her. "My baby," she says.

"Look at that old yellow thing standing out in that road," Gran'mon says. "What you ought to been done was got the sheriff on him for kidnap."

Me and Mama go back on the gallery.

"I been to Madame Toussaint's house," I say.

Mama looks at me and looks at Daddy out in the road. Daddy comes to the gate and looks at us on the gallery.

"Amy?" Daddy calls. "Can I speak to you a minute? Just one minute?"

"You don't get away from my gate, I'm go'n make that shotgun speak to you," Gran'mon says. "I didn't get you at twelve o'clock, but I won't miss you now."

"Amy, honey," Daddy calls. "Please."

"Come on, Sonny," Mama says.

"Where you going?" Gran'mon asks.

"Far as the gate," Mama says. "I'll talk to him. I reckon I owe him that much."

"You leave this house with that nigger, don't ever come back here again," Gran'mon says.

"You oughtn't talk like that, Rachel," Uncle Al says.

"I talk like I want," Gran'mon says. "She's my daughter; not yours, neither his."

Me and Mama go out to the gate where Daddy is. Daddy stands outside the gate and me and Mama stand inside.

"Lord, you look good, Amy," Daddy says. "Honey, didn't you miss me? Go on and say it. Go on and say how bad you missed me."

"That's all you want say to me?" Mama says.

"Honey, please," Daddy says. "Say you missed me. I been grieving all day like a dog."

"Come on, Sonny," Mama says. "Let's go back inside."

"Honey," Daddy says. "Please don't turn your back on me and go back to Freddie Jackson. Honey, I love you. I swear 'fore God I love you. Honey, you listening?"

"Come on, Sonny," Mama says.

"Honey," Daddy says, "if I burn the car like Madame Toussaint say, you'll come back home?"

"What?" Mama says.

"She say for Daddy—"

"Be still, Sonny," Mama says.

"She told me to set fire to it and you'll come back home," Daddy says. "You'll come back, honey?"

"She told you to burn up your car?" Mama says.

"If I want you to come back," Daddy says. "If I do it, you'll come back?"

"If you burn it up," Mama says. "If you burn it up, yes, I'll come back."

"Tonight?" Daddy says.

"Yes; tonight," Mama says.

"If I sold it?" Daddy says.

"Burn it," Mama says.

"I can get about fifty for it," Daddy says. "You could get couple dresses out of that."

"Burn it," Mama says. "You know what burn is?"

Daddy looks across the gate at Mama, and Mama looks right back at him. Daddy nods his head.

"I can't argue with you, honey," he says. "I'll go and burn it right now. You can come see if you want."

"No," Mama says, "I'll be here when you come back."

"Couldn't you go up home and start cooking some supper?" Daddy asks. "I'm just 's hungry as a dog."

"I'll cook when that car is burnt," Mama says. "Come on, Sonny."

"Can I go see Daddy burn his car, Mama?" I ask.

"No," Mama says. "You been in that cold long enough."

"I want see Daddy burn his car," I say. I start crying and stomping so Mama'll let me go.

"Let him go, honey," Daddy says. "I'll keep him warm."

"You can go," Mama says. "But don't come to me if you start that coughing tonight, you hear?"

"Uh-huh," I say.

Mama makes sure all my clothes's buttoned good, then she let me go. I run out in the road where Daddy is.

"I'll be back soon 's I can, honey," Daddy says. "And we'll straighten out everything, hear?"

"Just make sure you burn it," Mama says. "I'll find out."

"Honey, I'm go'n burn every bit of it," Daddy says.

"I'll be here when you come back," Mama says. "How you figuring on getting up there?"

"I'll go over and see if George Williams can't take me," Daddy says.

"I don't want Sonny in that cold too long," Mama says. "And you keep your hands in your pockets, Sonny."

"I ain't go'n take them out," I say.

Mama goes back up the walk toward the house. Daddy stands there just watching her.

"Lord, that's a sweet little woman," he says, shaking his head. "That's a sweet little woman you see going back to that house."

"Come on, Daddy," I say. "Let's go burn up the car."

Me and Daddy walk away from the fence.

"Let me get on your back and ride," I say.

"Can't you walk sometime," Daddy says. "What you think I'm educating you for—to treat me like a horse?"

5: Mr. George Williams drives his car to the side of the road, then we get out.

"Look like we got company," Mr. George Williams says.

Me and Daddy and Mr. George Williams go over where the people is. The people got a little fire burning, and some of them's sitting on the car fender. But most of them's standing round the little fire.

"Welcome," somebody says.

"Thanks," Daddy says. "Since this is my car you sitting on."

"Oh," the man says. He jumps up and the other two men jump up, too. They go over to the little fire and stand round it.

"We didn't mean no harm," one of them say.

Daddy goes over and peeps in the car. Then he opens the door and gets in. I go over to the car where he is.

"Go stand 'side the fire," Daddy says.

"I want get in with you," I say.

"Do what I tell you," Daddy says.

I go back to the fire, and I turn and look at Daddy in the car. Daddy passes his hand all over the car; then he just sit

67

there quiet-like. All the people round the fire look at Daddy in the car. I can hear them talking real low.

After a little while, Daddy opens the door and gets out. He comes over to the fire.

"Well," he says, "I guess that's it. You got a rope?"

"In the trunk," Mr. George Williams says. "What you go'n do, drag it off the highway?"

"We can't burn it out here," Daddy says.

"He say he go'n burn it," somebody at the fire says.

"I'm go'n burn it," Daddy says. "It's mine, ain't it?"

"Easy, Eddie," Mr. George Williams says.

Daddy is mad but he don't say any more. Mr. George Williams looks at Daddy, then he goes over to his car and gets the rope.

"Ought to be strong enough," Mr. George Williams says.

He hands Daddy the rope, then he goes and turns his car around. Everybody at the fire looks at Mr. George Williams backing up his car.

"Good," Daddy says.

Daddy gets between the cars and ties them together. Some of the people come over and watch him.

"Y'all got a side road anywhere round here?" he asks.

"Right over there," the man says. "Leads off back in the field. You ain't go'n burn up that good car for real, is you?"

"Who field this is?" Daddy asks.

"Mr. Roger Medlow," the man says.

"Any colored people got fields round here anywhere?" Daddy asks.

"Old man Ned Johnson 'bout two miles farther down the road," another man says.

"Why don't we just take it on back to the plantation?" Mr. George Williams says. "I doubt if Mr. Claude'll mind if we burnt it there."

"All right," Daddy says. "Might as well."

Me and Daddy get in his car. Some of the people from the

fire run up to Mr. George Williams's car. Mr. George Williams tells them something, and I see three of them jumping in. Mr. George Williams taps on the horn, then we get going. I sit 'way back in the seat and look at Daddy. Daddy's quiet. He's sorry because he got to burn up his car.

We go 'way down the road, then we turn and go down the quarter. Soon 's we get down there, I hear two of the men in Mr. George Williams's car calling to the people. I sit up in the seat and look out at them. They standing on the fenders, calling to the people.

"Come on," they saying. "Come on to the car-burning party. Free. Everybody welcome. Free."

We go farther down the quarter, and the two men keep on calling.

"Come on, everybody," one of them says.

"We having a car-burning party tonight," the other one says. "No charges."

The people start coming out on the galleries to see what all the racket is. I look back and I see some out in the yard, and some already out in the road. Mr. George Williams stops in front of Gran'mon's house.

"You go'n tell Amy?" he calls to Daddy. "Maybe she like to go, since you doing it all for her."

"Go tell your mama come on," Daddy says.

I jump out the car and run in the yard.

"Come on, everybody," one of the men says.

"We having a car-burning party tonight," the other one says. "Everybody invited. No charges."

I pull Gran'mon's door open and go in. Mama and Uncle Al and Gran'mon's sitting at the fireplace.

"Mama, Daddy say come on if you want see the burning," I say.

"See what burning?" Gran'mon asks. "Now don't tell me that crazy nigger going through with that."

"Come on, Mama," I say.

Mama and Uncle Al get up from the fireplace and go to the door.

"He sure got it out there," Uncle Al says.

"Come on, Mama," I say. "Come on, Uncle Al."

"Wait till I get my coat," Mama says. "Mama, you going?"

"I ain't missing this for the world," Gran'mon says. "I still think he's bluffing."

Gran'mon gets her coat and Uncle Al gets his coat; then we go on outside. Plenty people standing round Daddy's car now. I can see more people opening doors and coming out on the galleries.

"Get in," Daddy says. "Sorry I can't take but two. Mama, you want ride?"

"No, thanks," Gran'mon says. "You might just get it in your head to run off in that canal with me in there. Let your wife and child ride. I'll walk with the rest of the people."

"Get in, honey," Daddy says. "It's getting cold out there."

Mama takes my arm and helps me in; then she gets in and shuts the door.

"How far down you going?" Uncle Al asks.

"Near the sugar house," Daddy says. He taps on the horn and Mr. George Williams drives away.

"Come on, everybody," one of the men says.

"We having a car-burning party tonight," the other one says. "Everybody invited."

Mr. George Williams drives his car over the railroad tracks. I look back and I see plenty people following Daddy's car. I can't see Uncle Al and Gran'mon, but I know they back there, too.

We keep going. We get almost to the sugar house, then we turn down another road. The other road is bumpy and I have to bounce on the seat.

"Well, I reckon this's it," Daddy says.

Mama don't say nothing to Daddy.

"You know it ain't too late to change your mind," Daddy says. "All I got to do is stop George and untie the car."

"You brought matches?" Mama asks.

"All right," Daddy says. "All right. Don't start fussing."

We go a little farther and Daddy taps on the horn. Mr. George Williams stops his car. Daddy gets out his car and go and talk with Mr. George Williams. Little bit later I see Daddy coming back.

"Y'all better get out here," he says. "We go'n take it down the field a piece."

Me and Mama get out. I look down the headland and I see Uncle Al and Gran'mon and all the other people coming. Some of them even got flashlights because it's getting dark now. They come where me and Mama's standing. I look down the field and I see the cars going down the row. It's dark, but Mr. George Williams got bright lights on his car. The cars stop and Daddy get out his car and go and untie the rope. Mr. George Williams goes and turns around and come back to the headland where all the people standing. Then he turns his lights on Daddy's car so everybody can see the burning. I see Daddy getting some gas out the tank.

"Give me a hand down here," Daddy calls. But that don't even sound like Daddy's voice.

Plenty people run down the field to help Daddy. They get round the car and start shaking it. I see the car leaning; then it tips over.

"Well," Gran'mon says. "I never would've thought it."

I see Daddy going all round the car with the can, then I see him splashing some inside the car. All the other people back back to give him room. I see Daddy scratching a match and throwing it in the car. He scratches another one and throw that one in the car, too. I see little bit fire, then I see plenty.

"I just do declare," Gran'mon says. "I must be dreaming. He's a man after all."

Gran'mon the only person talking; everybody else is quiet. We stay there a long time and look at the fire. The fire burns down and Daddy and them go and look at the car again. Daddy picks up the can and pours some more gas on the fire. The fire gets big. We look at the fire some more.

"Never thought that was in Eddie," somebody says real low.

"You not the only one," somebody else says.

"He loved that car more than he loved anything."

"No, he must love her more," another person says.

The fire burns down again. Daddy and them go and look at the car. They stay there a good while, then they come out to the headland where we standing.

"What's that, George?" Mama asks.

"The pump," Mr. George Williams says. "Eddie gave it to me for driving him to get his car."

"Hand it here," Mama says.

Mr. George Williams looks at Daddy, but he hands the pump to Mama. Mama goes on down the field with the pump and throws it in the fire. I watch Mama coming back.

"When Eddie gets paid Saturday he'll pay you," Mama says. "You ready to go home, Eddie?"

Daddy nods his head.

"Sonny," Mama says.

I go where Mama is and Mama takes my hand. Daddy raises his head and looks at the people standing round looking at us.

"Thank y'all," he says.

Me and Mama go in Gran'mon's house and pull the big bundle out on the gallery. Daddy picks the bundle up and puts it on his head, then we go up the quarter to us house. Mama opens the gate and me and Daddy go in. We go inside and Mama lights the lamp.

"You hungry?" Mama asks Daddy.

"How can you ask that?" Daddy says. "I'm starving."

"You want eat now or after you whip me?" Mama says.

"Whip you?" Daddy asks. "What I'm go'n be whipping you for?"

Mama goes back in the kitchen. She don't find what she's looking for, and I hear her going outside.

"Where Mama going, Daddy?"

"Don't ask me," Daddy says. "I don't know no more than you."

Daddy gets some kindling out of the corner and puts it in the fireplace. Then he pours some coal oil on the kindling and lights a match to it. Me and Daddy squat down on the fireplace and watch the fire burning.

I hear the back door shut, then I see Mama coming in the front room. Mama's got a great big old switch.

"Here," she says.

"What's that for?" Daddy says.

"Here. Take it," Mama says.

"I ain't got nothing to beat you for, Amy," Daddy says.

"You whip me," Mama says, "or I turn right round and walk on out that door."

Daddy stands up and looks at Mama.

"You must be crazy," Daddy says. "Stop all that foolishness, Amy, and go cook me some food."

"Get your pot, Sonny," Mama says.

"Shucks," I say. "Now where we going? I'm getting tired walking in all that cold. 'Fore you know it I'm go'n have whooping cough."

"Get your pot and stop answering me back, boy," Mama says.

I go to my bed and pick up the pot again.

"Shucks," I say.

"You ain't leaving here," Daddy says.

"You better stop me," Mama says, going to the bundle.

"All right," Daddy says. "I'll beat you if that's what you want."

Daddy gets the switch off the floor and I start crying.

"Lord, have mercy," Daddy says. "Now what?"

"Whip me," Mama says.

"Amy, whip you for what?" Daddy says. "Amy, please, just go back there and cook me something to eat."

"Come on, Sonny," Mama says. "Let's get out of this house."

"All right," Daddy says. Daddy hits Mama two times on the legs. "That's enough," he says.

"Beat me," Mama says.

I cry some more. "Don't beat my mama," I say. "I don't want you to beat my mama."

"Sonny, please," Daddy says. "What y'all trying to do to me—run me crazy? I burnt up the car—ain't that enough?"

"I'm just go'n tell you one more time," Mama says.

"All right," Daddy says. "I'm go'n beat you if that's what you want."

Daddy starts beating Mama, and I cry some more; but Daddy don't stop beating her.

"Beat me harder," Mama says. "I mean it. I mean it."

"Honey, please," Daddy says.

"You better do it," Mama says. "I mean it."

Daddy keeps on beating Mama, and Mama cries and goes down on her knees.

"Leave my mama alone, you old yellow dog," I say. "You leave my mama alone." I throw the pot at him but I miss him, and the pot go bouncing 'cross the floor.

Daddy throws the switch away and runs to Mama and picks her up. He takes Mama to the bed and begs her to stop crying. I get on my own bed and cry in the cover.

I feel somebody shaking me, and I must've been sleeping.

"Wake up," I hear Daddy saying.

I'm tired and I don't feel like getting up. I feel like sleeping some more.

"You want some supper?" Daddy asks.

"Uh-huh."

"Get up then," Daddy says.

I get up. I got all my clothes on and my shoes on.

"It's morning?" I ask.

"No," Daddy says. "Still night. Come on back in the kitchen and eat supper."

I follow Daddy in the kitchen and me and him sit down at the table. Mama brings the food to the table and she sits down, too.

"Bless this food, Father, which we're about to receive, the nurse of our bodies, for Christ sake, amen," Mama says.

I raise my head and look at Mama. I can see where she's been crying. Her face is all swole. I look at Daddy and he's eating. Mama and Daddy don't talk, and I don't say nothing, either. I eat my food. We eating sweet potatoes and bread. I'm having a glass of clabber, too.

"What a day," Daddy says.

Mama don't say nothing. She's just picking over her food.

"Mad?" Daddy says.

"No," Mama says.

"Honey?" Daddy says.

Mama looks at him.

"I didn't beat you because you did us thing with Freddie Jackson, did I?" Daddy says.

"No," Mama says.

"Well, why then?" Daddy says.

"Because I don't want you to be the laughingstock of the plantation," Mama says.

"Who go'n laugh at me?" Daddy says.

"Everybody," Mama says. "Mama and all. Now they don't have nothing to laugh about."

"Honey, I don't mind if they laugh at me," Daddy says.

"I do mind," Mama says.

"Did I hurt you?"

"I'm all right," she says.

"You ain't mad no more?" Daddy says.

"No," Mama says. "I'm not mad."

Mama picks up a little bit of food and puts it in her mouth.

"Finish eating your supper, Sonny," she says.

"I got enough," I say.

"Drink your clabber," Mama says.

I drink all my clabber and show Mama the glass.

"Go get your book," Mama says. "It's on the dresser."

I go in the front room to get my book.

"One of us got to go to school with him tomorrow," I hear Mama saying. I see her handing Daddy the note. Daddy waves it back. "Here," she says.

"Honey, you know I don't know how to act in no place like that," Daddy says.

"Time to learn," Mama says. She gives Daddy the note. "What page your lesson on, Sonny?"

I turn to the page, and I lean on Mama's leg and let her carry me over my lesson. Mama holds the book in her hand. She carries me over my lesson two times, then she makes me point to some words and spell some words.

"He knows it," Daddy says.

"I'll take you over it again tomorrow morning," Mama says. "Don't let me forget it now."

"Uh-uh."

"Your daddy'll carry you over it tomorrow night," Mama says. "One night me, one night you."

"With no car," Daddy says, "I reckon I'll be round plenty now. You think we'll ever get another one, honey?"

Daddy's picking in his teeth with a broom straw.

"When you learn how to act with one," Mama says. "I ain't got nothing against cars."

"I guess you right, honey," Daddy says. "I was going little too far."

"It's time for bed, Sonny," Mama says. "Go in the front room and say your prayers to your daddy."

Me and Daddy leave Mama back there in the kitchen. I put my book on the dresser and I go to the fireplace where Daddy is. Daddy puts another piece of wood on the fire and plenty sparks shoot up in the chimley. Daddy helps me to take off my clothes. I kneel down and lean against his leg.

"Start off," Daddy says. "I'll catch you if you miss something."

"Lay me down to sleep," I say. "I pray the Lord my soul to keep. If I should die before I wake, I pray the Lord my soul to take. God bless Mama and Daddy. God bless Gran'mon and Uncle Al. God bless the church. God bless Miss Hebert. God bless Bill and Juanita." I hear Daddy gaping. "God bless everybody else. Amen."

I jump up off my knees. Them bricks on the fireplace make my knees hurt.

"Did you tell God to bless Johnny Green and Madame Toussaint?" Daddy says.

"No," I say.

"Get down there and tell Him to bless them, too," Daddy says.

"Old Rollo, too?"

"That's up to you and Him for that," Daddy says. "Get back down there."

I get back on my knees. I don't get on the bricks because they make my knees hurt. I get on the floor and lean against the chair.

"And God bless Mr. Johnny Green and Madame Toussaint," I say.

77

"All right," Daddy says. "Warm up good."

Daddy goes over to my bed and pulls the cover back.

"Come on," he says. "Jump in."

I run and jump in the bed. Daddy pulls the cover up to my neck.

"Good night, Daddy."

"Good night," Daddy says.

"Good night, Mama."

"Good night, Sonny," Mama says.

I turn on my side and look at Daddy at the fireplace. Mama comes out of the kitchen and goes to the fireplace. Mama warms up good and goes to the bundle.

"Leave it alone," Daddy says. "We'll get up early tomorrow and get it."

"I'm going to bed," Mama says. "You coming now?"

"Uh-hunnnnn," Daddy says.

Mama comes to my bed and tucks the cover under me good. She leans over and kisses me and tucks the cover some more. She goes over to the bundle and gets her nightgown, then she goes in the kitchen and puts it on. She comes back and puts her clothes she took off on a chair 'side the wall. Mama kneels down and says her prayers, then she gets in the bed and covers up. Daddy stands up and takes off his clothes. I see Daddy in his big old long white BVD's. Daddy blows out the lamp, and I hear the spring when Daddy gets in the bed. Daddy never says his prayers.

"Sleepy?" Daddy says.

"Uh-uhnnn," Mama says.

I hear the spring. I hear Mama and Daddy talking low, but I don't know what they saying. I go to sleep some, but I open my eyes again. It's some dark in the room. I hear Mama and Daddy talking low. I like Mama and Daddy. I like Uncle Al, but I don't like old Gran'mon too much. Gran'mon's always talking bad about Daddy. I don't like old Mr. Freddie

Jackson, either. Mama say she didn't do her and Daddy's thing with Mr. Freddie Jackson. I like Mr. George Williams. We went riding 'way up the road with Mr. George Williams. We got Daddy's car and brought it all the way back here. Daddy and them turned the car over and Daddy poured some gas on it and set it on fire. Daddy ain't got no more car now. . . . I know my lesson. I ain't go'n wee-wee on myself no more. Daddy's going to school with me tomorrow. I'm go'n show him I can beat Billy Joe Martin shooting marbles. I can shoot all over Billy Joe Martin. And I can beat him running, too. He thinks he can run fast. I'm go'n show Daddy I can beat him running. . . . I don't know why I had to say, "God bless Madame Toussaint." I don't like her. And I don't like old Rollo, either. Rollo can bark some loud. He made my head hurt with all that loud barking. Madame Toussaint's old house don't smell good. Us house smell good. I hear the spring on Mama and Daddy's bed. I get 'way under the cover. I go to sleep little bit, but I wake up. I go to sleep some more. I hear the spring on Mama and Daddy's bed. I hear it plenty now. It's some dark under here. It's warm. I feel good 'way under here.

The Sky Is Gray

THE SKY IS GRAY

I: Go'n be coming in a few minutes. Coming round that bend down there full speed. And I'm go'n get out my handkerchief and wave it down, and we go'n get on it and go.

I keep on looking for it, but Mama don't look that way no more. She's looking down the road where we just come from. It's a long old road, and far 's you can see you don't see nothing but gravel. You got dry weeds on both sides, and you got trees on both sides, and fences on both sides, too. And you got cows in the pastures and they standing close together. And when we was coming out here to catch the bus I seen the smoke coming out of the cows's noses.

I look at my mama and I know what she's thinking. I been with Mama so much, just me and her, I know what she's thinking all the time. Right now it's home—Auntie and them. She's thinking if they got enough wood—if she left enough there to keep them warm till we get back. She's thinking if it go'n rain and if any of them go'n have to go out in the rain. She's thinking 'bout the hog—if he go'n get out, and if Ty and Val be able to get him back in. She always worry like that when she leaves the house. She don't worry too much if she leave me there with the smaller ones, 'cause she know I'm go'n look after them and look after Auntie and everything else. I'm the oldest and she say I'm the man.

I look at my mama and I love my mama. She's wearing that black coat and that black hat and she's looking sad. I love my mama and I want put my arm round her and tell her. But I'm not supposed to do that. She say that's weakness and that's crybaby stuff, and she don't want no crybaby round her. She don't want you to be scared, either. 'Cause Ty's scared of ghosts and she's always whipping him. I'm scared of the dark, too, but I make 'tend I ain't. I make 'tend I ain't 'cause I'm the oldest, and I got to set a good sample for the rest. I can't ever be scared and I can't ever cry. And that's why I never said nothing 'bout my teeth. It's been hurting me and hurting me close to a month now, but I never said it. I didn't say it 'cause I didn't want act like a crybaby, and 'cause I know we didn't have enough money to go have it pulled. But, Lord, it been hurting me. And look like it wouldn't start till at night when you was trying to get yourself little sleep. Then soon 's you shut your eyes—ummm-ummm, Lord, look like it go right down to your heartstring.

"Hurting, hanh?" Ty'd say.

I'd shake my head, but I wouldn't open my mouth for nothing. You open your mouth and let that wind in, and it almost kill you.

I'd just lay there and listen to them snore. Ty there, right 'side me, and Auntie and Val over by the fireplace. Val younger than me and Ty, and he sleeps with Auntie. Mama sleeps round the other side with Louis and Walker.

I'd just lay there and listen to them, and listen to that wind out there, and listen to that fire in the fireplace. Sometimes it'd stop long enough to let me get little rest. Sometimes it just hurt, hurt, hurt. Lord, have mercy.

2: Auntie knowed it was hurting me. I didn't tell nobody but Ty, 'cause we buddies and he ain't go'n tell nobody. But some kind of way Auntie found out. When she asked me, I told her no, nothing was wrong. But she knowed it all the time. She told me to mash up a piece of aspirin and wrap it in some cotton and jugg it down in that hole. I did it, but it didn't do no good. It stopped for a little while, and started right back again. Auntie wanted to tell Mama, but I told her, "Uh-uh." 'Cause I knowed we didn't have any money, and it just was go'n make her mad again. So Auntie told Monsieur Bayonne, and Monsieur Bayonne came over to the house and told me to kneel down 'side him on the fireplace. He put his finger in his mouth and made the Sign of the Cross on my jaw. The tip of Monsieur Bayonne's finger is some hard, 'cause he's always playing on that guitar. If we sit outside at night we can always hear Monsieur Bayonne playing on his guitar. Sometimes we leave him out there playing on the guitar.

Monsieur Bayonne made the Sign of the Cross over and over on my jaw, but that didn't do no good. Even when he prayed and told me to pray some, too, that tooth still hurt me.

"How you feeling?" he say.

"Same," I say.

He kept on praying and making the Sign of the Cross and I kept on praying, too.

"Still hurting?" he say.

"Yes, sir."

Monsieur Bayonne mashed harder and harder on my jaw. He mashed so hard he almost pushed me over on Ty. But then he stopped.

"What kind of prayers you praying, boy?" he say.

"Baptist," I say.

"Well, I'll be—no wonder that tooth still killing him. I'm going one way and he pulling the other. Boy, don't you know any Catholic prayers?"

"I know 'Hail Mary,' " I say.

"Then you better start saying it."

"Yes, sir."

He started mashing on my jaw again, and I could hear him praying at the same time. And, sure enough, after while it stopped hurting me.

Me and Ty went outside where Monsieur Bayonne's two hounds was and we started playing with them. "Let's go hunting," Ty say. "All right," I say; and we went on back in the pasture. Soon the hounds got on a trail, and me and Ty followed them all 'cross the pasture and then back in the woods, too. And then they cornered this little old rabbit and killed him, and me and Ty made them get back, and we picked up the rabbit and started on back home. But my tooth had started hurting me again. It was hurting me plenty now, but I wouldn't tell Monsieur Bayonne. That night I didn't sleep a bit, and first thing in the morning Auntie told me to go back and let Monsieur Bayonne pray over me some more. Monsieur Bayonne was in his kitchen making coffee when I got there. Soon 's he seen me he knowed what was wrong.

"All right, kneel down there 'side that stove," he say. "And this time make sure you pray Catholic. I don't know nothing 'bout that Baptist, and I don't want know nothing 'bout him."

3: Last night Mama say, "Tomorrow we going to town."

"It ain't hurting me no more," I say. "I can eat anything on it."

"Tomorrow we going to town," she say.

And after she finished eating, she got up and went to bed.

She always go to bed early now. 'Fore Daddy went in the Army, she used to stay up late. All of us sitting out on the gallery or round the fire. But now, look like soon 's she finish eating she go to bed.

This morning when I woke up, her and Auntie was standing 'fore the fireplace. She say: "Enough to get there and get back. Dollar and a half to have it pulled. Twenty-five for me to go, twenty-five for him. Twenty-five for me to come back, twenty-five for him. Fifty cents left. Guess I get little piece of salt meat with that."

"Sure can use it," Auntie say. "White beans and no salt meat ain't white beans."

"I do the best I can," Mama say.

They was quiet after that, and I made 'tend I was still asleep.

"James, hit the floor," Auntie say.

I still made 'tend I was asleep. I didn't want them to know I was listening.

"All right," Auntie say, shaking me by the shoulder. "Come on. Today's the day."

I pushed the cover down to get out, and Ty grabbed it and pulled it back.

"You, too, Ty," Auntie say.

"I ain't getting no teef pulled," Ty say.

"Don't mean it ain't time to get up," Auntie say. "Hit it, Ty."

Ty got up grumbling.

"James, you hurry up and get in your clothes and eat your food," Auntie say. "What time y'all coming back?" she say to Mama.

"That 'leven o'clock bus," Mama say. "Got to get back in that field this evening."

"Get a move on you, James," Auntie say.

I went in the kitchen and washed my face, then I ate my

breakfast. I was having bread and syrup. The bread was warm and hard and tasted good. And I tried to make it last a long time.

Ty came back there grumbling and mad at me.

"Got to get up," he say. "I ain't having no teefes pulled. What I got to be getting up for?"

Ty poured some syrup in his pan and got a piece of bread. He didn't wash his hands, neither his face, and I could see that white stuff in his eyes.

"You the one getting your teef pulled," he say. "What I got to get up for. I bet if I was getting a teef pulled, you wouldn't be getting up. Shucks; syrup again. I'm getting tired of this old syrup. Syrup, syrup, syrup. I'm go'n take with the sugar diabetes. I want me some bacon sometime."

"Go out in the field and work and you can have your bacon," Auntie say. She stood in the middle door looking at Ty. "You better be glad you got syrup. Some people ain't got that—hard 's time is."

"Shucks," Ty say. "How can I be strong."

"I don't know too much 'bout your strength," Auntie say; "but I know where you go'n be hot at, you keep that grumbling up. James, get a move on you; your mama waiting."

I ate my last piece of bread and went in the front room. Mama was standing 'fore the fireplace warming her hands. I put on my coat and my cap, and we left the house.

4: I look down there again, but it still ain't coming. I almost say, "It ain't coming yet," but I keep my mouth shut. 'Cause that's something else she don't like. She don't like for you to say something just for nothing. She can see it ain't coming, I can see it ain't coming, so why say it ain't coming. I don't say it, I turn and look at the river that's back of us. It's so cold the smoke's just raising up from the water. I see a bunch of pool-doos not too far out—just on the other side the lilies. I'm wondering if you can eat pool-doos. I ain't too sure, 'cause I ain't never ate none. But I done ate owls and blackbirds, and I done ate redbirds, too. I didn't want kill the redbirds, but she made me kill them. They had two of them back there. One in my trap, one in Ty's trap. Me and Ty was go'n play with them and let them go, but she made me kill them 'cause we needed the food.

"I can't," I say. "I can't."

"Here," she say. "Take it."

"I can't," I say. "I can't. I can't kill him, Mama, please."

"Here," she say. "Take this fork, James."

"Please, Mama, I can't kill him," I say.

I could tell she was go'n hit me. I jerked back, but I didn't jerk back soon enough.

"Take it," she say.

I took it and reached in for him, but he kept on hopping to the back.

"I can't, Mama," I say. The water just kept on running down my face. "I can't," I say.

"Get him out of there," she say.

I reached in for him and he kept on hopping to the back. Then I reached in farther, and he pecked me on the hand.

"I can't, Mama," I say.

She slapped me again.

I reached in again, but he kept on hopping out my way. Then he hopped to one side and I reached there. The fork got him on the leg and I heard his leg pop. I pulled my hand out 'cause I had hurt him.

"Give it here," she say, and jerked the fork out my hand.

She reached in and got the little bird right in the neck. I heard the fork go in his neck, and I heard it go in the ground. She brought him out and helt him right in front of me.

"That's one," she say. She shook him off and gived me the fork. "Get the other one."

89

"I can't, Mama," I say. "I'll do anything, but don't make me do that."

She went to the corner of the fence and broke the biggest switch over there she could find. I knelt 'side the trap, crying.

"Get him out of there," she say.

"I can't, Mama."

She started hitting me 'cross the back. I went down on the ground, crying.

"Get him," she say.

"Octavia?" Auntie say.

'Cause she had come out of the house and she was standing by the tree looking at us.

"Get him out of there," Mama say.

"Octavia," Auntie say, "explain to him. Explain to him. Just don't beat him. Explain to him."

But she hit me and hit me and hit me.

I'm still young—I ain't no more than eight; but I know now; I know why I had to do it. (They was so little, though. They was so little. I 'member how I picked the feathers off them and cleaned them and helt them over the fire. Then we all ate them. Ain't had but a little bitty piece each, but we all had a little bitty piece, and everybody just looked at me 'cause they was so proud.) Suppose she had to go away? That's why I had to do it. Suppose she had to go away like Daddy went away? Then who was go'n look after us? They had to be somebody left to carry on. I didn't know it then, but I know it now. Auntie and Monsieur Bayonne talked to me and made me see.

5: Time I see it I get out my handkerchief and start waving. It's still 'way down there, but I keep waving anyhow. Then it come up and stop and me and Mama get on. Mama tell me go sit in the back while she pay. I do like she say, and the people look at me. When I pass the little sign that say "White" and "Colored," I start looking for a seat. I just see one of them back there, but I don't take it, 'cause I want my mama to sit down herself. She comes in the back and sit down, and I lean on the seat. They got seats in the front, but I know I can't sit there, 'cause I have to sit back of the sign. Anyhow, I don't want sit there if my mama go'n sit back here.

They got a lady sitting 'side my mama and she looks at me and smiles little bit. I smile back, but I don't open my mouth, 'cause the wind'll get in and make that tooth ache. The lady take out a pack of gum and reach me a slice, but I shake my head. The lady just can't understand why a little boy'll turn down gum, and she reach me a slice again. This time I point to my jaw. The lady understands and smiles little bit, and I smile little bit, but I don't open my mouth, though.

They got a girl sitting 'cross from me. She got on a red overcoat and her hair's plaited in one big plait. First, I make 'tend I don't see her over there, but then I start looking at her little bit. She make 'tend she don't see me, either, but I catch her looking that way. She got a cold, and every now and then she h'ist that little handkerchief to her nose. She ought to blow it, but she don't. Must think she's too much a lady or something.

Every time she h'ist that little handkerchief, the lady 'side her say something in her ear. She shakes her head and lays her hands in her lap again. Then I catch her kind of looking where I'm at. I smile at her little bit. But think she'll smile back? Uh-uh. She just turn up her little old nose and turn her head. Well, I show her both of us can turn us head. I turn mine too and look out at the river.

The river is gray. The sky is gray. They have pool-doos on the water. The water is wavy, and the pool-doos go up and down. The bus go round a turn, and you got plenty trees hiding the river. Then the bus go round another turn, and I can see the river again.

I look toward the front where all the white people sitting. Then I look at that little old gal again. I don't look right at her, 'cause I don't want all them people to know I love her. I just look at her little bit, like I'm looking out that window over there. But she knows I'm looking that way, and she kind of look at me, too. The lady sitting 'side her catch her this time, and she leans over and says something in her ear.

"I don't love him nothing," that little old gal says out loud.

Everybody back there hear her mouth, and all of them look at us and laugh.

"I don't love you, either," I say. "So you don't have to turn up your nose, Miss."

"You the one looking," she say.

"I wasn't looking at you," I say. "I was looking out that window, there."

"Out that window, my foot," she say. "I seen you. Everytime I turned round you was looking at me."

"You must of been looking yourself if you seen me all them times," I say.

"Shucks," she say, "I got me all kind of boyfriends."

"I got girlfriends, too," I say.

"Well, I just don't want you getting your hopes up," she say.

I don't say no more to that little old gal 'cause I don't want have to bust her in the mouth. I lean on the seat where Mama sitting, and I don't even look that way no more. When we get to Bayonne, she jugg her little old tongue out at me. I make 'tend I'm go'n hit her, and she duck down 'side her mama. And all the people laugh at us again.

92

spone stream of consciousness

6: Me and Mama get off and start walking in town. Bay-
onne is a little bitty town. Baton Rouge is a hundred
times bigger than Bayonne. I went to Baton Rouge
once—me, Ty, Mama, and Daddy. But that was 'way back
yonder, 'fore Daddy went in the Army. I wonder when we
go'n see him again. I wonder when. Look like he ain't ever
coming back home. . . . Even the pavement all cracked in
Bayonne. Got grass shooting right out the sidewalk. Got
weeds in the ditch, too; just like they got at home.

It's some cold in Bayonne. Look like it's colder than it is
home. The wind blows in my face, and I feel that stuff run-
ning down my nose. I sniff. Mama says use that handkerchief.
I blow my nose and put it back.

We pass a school and I see them white children playing in
the yard. Big old red school, and them children just running
and playing. Then we pass a café, and I see a bunch of people
in there eating. I wish I was in there 'cause I'm cold. Mama
tells me keep my eyes in front where they belong.

We pass stores that's got dummies, and we pass another
café, and then we pass a shoe shop, and that bald-head man in
there fixing on a shoe. I look at him and I butt into that white
lady, and Mama jerks me in front and tells me stay there.

We come up to the courthouse, and I see the flag waving
there. This flag ain't like the one we got at school. This one
here ain't got but a handful of stars. One at school got a big
pile of stars—one for every state. We pass it and we turn and
there it is—the dentist office. Me and Mama go in, and they
got people sitting everywhere you look. They even got a little
boy in there younger than me.

Me and Mama sit on that bench, and a white lady come in
there and ask me what my name is. Mama tells her and the
white lady goes on back. Then I hear somebody hollering in
there. Soon 's that little boy hear him hollering, he starts

hollering, too. His mama pats him and pats him, trying to make him hush up, but he ain't thinking 'bout his mama.

The man that was hollering in there comes out holding his jaw. He is a big old man and he's wearing overalls and a jumper.

"Got it, hanh?" another man asks him.

The man shakes his head—don't want open his mouth.

"Man, I thought they was killing you in there," the other man says. "Hollering like a pig under a gate."

The man don't say nothing. He just heads for the door, and the other man follows him.

"John Lee," the white lady says. "John Lee Williams."

The little boy juggs his head down in his mama's lap and holler more now. His mama tells him go with the nurse, but he ain't thinking 'bout his mama. His mama tells him again, but he don't even hear her. His mama picks him up and takes him in there, and even when the white lady shuts the door I can still hear little old John Lee.

"I often wonder why the Lord let a child like that suffer," a lady says to my mama. The lady's sitting right in front of us on another bench. She's got on a white dress and a black sweater. She must be a nurse or something herself, I reckon.

"Not us to question," a man says.

"Sometimes I don't know if we shouldn't," the lady says.

"I know definitely we shouldn't," the man says. The man looks like a preacher. He's big and fat and he's got on a black suit. He's got a gold chain, too.

"Why?" the lady says.

"Why anything?" the preacher says.

"Yes," the lady says. "Why anything?"

"Not us to question," the preacher says.

The lady looks at the preacher a little while and looks at Mama again.

"And look like it's the poor who suffers the most," she says. "I don't understand it."

"Best not to even try," the preacher says. "He works in mysterious ways—wonders to perform."

Right then little John Lee bust out hollering, and everybody turn they head to listen.

"He's not a good dentist," the lady says. "Dr. Robillard is much better. But more expensive. That's why most of the colored people come here. The white people go to Dr. Robillard. Y'all from Bayonne?"

"Down the river," my mama says. And that's all she go'n say, 'cause she don't talk much. But the lady keeps on looking at her, and so she says, "Near Morgan."

"I see," the lady says.

7: "That's the trouble with the black people in this country today," somebody else says. This one here's sitting on the same side me and Mama's sitting, and he is kind of sitting in front of that preacher. He looks like a teacher or somebody that goes to college. He's got on a suit, and he's got a book that he's been reading. "We don't question is exactly our problem," he says. "We should question and question and question—question everything."

The preacher just looks at him a long time. He done put a toothpick or something in his mouth, and he just keeps on turning it and turning it. You can see he don't like that boy with that book.

"Maybe you can explain what you mean," he says.

"I said what I meant," the boy says. "Question everything. Every stripe, every star, every word spoken. Everything."

"It 'pears to me that this young lady and I was talking 'bout God, young man," the preacher says.

"Question Him, too," the boy says.

"Wait," the preacher says. "Wait now."

"You heard me right," the boy says. "His existence as well as everything else. Everything."

The preacher just looks across the room at the boy. You can see he's getting madder and madder. But mad or no mad, the boy ain't thinking 'bout him. He looks at that preacher just 's hard 's the preacher looks at him.

"Is this what they coming to?" the preacher says. "Is this what we educating them for?"

"You're not educating me," the boy says. "I wash dishes at night so that I can go to school in the day. So even the words you spoke need questioning."

The preacher just looks at him and shakes his head.

"When I come in this room and seen you there with your book, I said to myself, 'There's an intelligent man.' How wrong a person can be."

"Show me one reason to believe in the existence of a God," the boys says.

"My heart tells me," the preacher says.

"'My heart tells me,'" the boys says. "'My heart tells me.' Sure, 'My heart tells me.' And as long as you listen to what your heart tells you, you will have only what the white man gives you and nothing more. Me, I don't listen to my heart. The purpose of the heart is to pump blood throughout the body, and nothing else."

"Who's your paw, boy?" the preacher says.

"Why?"

"Who is he?"

"He's dead."

"And your mom?"

"She's in Charity Hospital with pneumonia. Half killed herself, working for nothing."

"And 'cause he's dead and she's sick, you mad at the world?"

"I'm not mad at the world. I'm questioning the world. I'm questioning it with cold logic, sir. What do words like Freedom, Liberty, God, White, Colored mean? I want to know. That's why *you* are sending us to school, to read and to ask questions. And because we ask these questions, you call us mad. No sir, it is not us who are mad."

"You keep saying 'us'?"

" 'Us.' Yes—us. I'm not alone."

The preacher just shakes his head. Then he looks at everybody in the room—everybody. Some of the people look down at the floor, keep from looking at him. I kind of look 'way myself, but soon 's I know he done turn his head, I look that way again.

"I'm sorry for you," he says to the boy.

"Why?" the boy says. "Why not be sorry for yourself? Why are you so much better off than I am? Why aren't you sorry for these other people in here? Why not be sorry for the lady who had to drag her child into the dentist office? Why not be sorry for the lady sitting on that bench over there? Be sorry for them. Not for me. Some way or the other I'm going to make it."

"No, I'm sorry for you," the preacher says.

"Of course, of course," the boy says, nodding his head. "You're sorry for me because I rock that pillar you're leaning on."

"You can't ever rock the pillar I'm leaning on, young man. It's stronger than anything man can ever do."

"You believe in God because a man told you to believe in God," the boy says. "A white man told you to believe in God. And why? To keep you ignorant so he can keep his feet on your neck."

"So now we the ignorant?" the preacher says.

"Yes," the boy says. "Yes." And he opens his book again. The preacher just looks at him sitting there. The boy done forgot all about him. Everybody else make 'tend they done forgot the squabble, too.

Then I see that preacher getting up real slow. Preacher's a great big old man and he got to brace himself to get up. He comes over where the boy is sitting. He just stands there a little while looking down at him, but the boy don't raise his head.

"Get up, boy," preacher says.

The boy looks up at him, then he shuts his book real slow and stands up. Preacher just hauls back and hit him in the face. The boy falls back 'gainst the wall, but he straightens himself up and looks right back at that preacher.

"You forgot the other cheek," he says.

The preacher hauls back and hit him again on the other side. But this time the boy braces himself and don't fall.

"That hasn't changed a thing," he says.

The preacher just looks at the boy. The preacher's breathing real hard like he just run up a big hill. The boy sits down and opens his book again.

"I feel sorry for you," the preacher says. "I never felt so sorry for a man before."

The boy makes 'tend he don't even hear that preacher. He keeps on reading his book. The preacher goes back and gets his hat off the chair.

"Excuse me," he says to us. "I'll come back some other time. Y'all, please excuse me."

And he looks at the boy and goes out the room. The boy h'ist his hand up to his mouth one time to wipe 'way some blood. All the rest of the time he keeps on reading. And nobody else in there say a word.

8: Little John Lee and his mama come out the dentist office, and the nurse calls somebody else in. Then little bit later they come out, and the nurse calls another name.

But fast 's she calls somebody in there, somebody else comes in the place where we sitting, and the room stays full.

The people coming in now, all of them wearing big coats. One of them says something 'bout sleeting, another one says he hope not. Another one says he think it ain't nothing but rain. 'Cause, he says, rain can get awful cold this time of year.

All round the room they talking. Some of them talking to people right by them, some of them talking to people clear 'cross the room, some of them talking to anybody'll listen. It's a little bitty room, no bigger than us kitchen, and I can see everybody in there. The little old room's full of smoke, 'cause you got two old men smoking pipes over by that side door. I think I feel my tooth thumping me some, and I hold my breath and wait. I wait and wait, but it don't thump me no more. Thank God for that.

I feel like going to sleep, and I lean back 'gainst the wall. But I'm scared to go to sleep. Scared 'cause the nurse might call my name and I won't hear her. And Mama might go to sleep, too, and she'll be mad if neither one of us heard the nurse.

I look up at Mama. I love my mama. I love my mama. And when cotton come I'm go'n get her a new coat. And I ain't go'n get a black one, either. I think I'm go'n get her a red one.

"They got some books over there," I say. "Want read one of them?"

Mama looks at the books, but she don't answer me.

"You got yourself a little man there," the lady says.

Mama don't say nothing to the lady, but she must've smiled, 'cause I seen the lady smiling back. The lady looks at me a little while, like she's feeling sorry for me.

"You sure got that preacher out here in a hurry," she says to that boy.

The boy looks up at her and looks in his book again.

When I grow up I want be just like him. I want clothes like that and I want keep a book with me, too.

"You really don't believe in God?" the lady says.

"No," he says.

"But why?" the lady says.

"Because the wind is pink," he says.

"What?" the lady says.

The boy don't answer her no more. He just reads in his book.

"Talking 'bout the wind is pink," that old lady says. She's sitting on the same bench with the boy and she's trying to look in his face. The boy makes 'tend the old lady ain't even there. He just keeps on reading. "Wind is pink," she says again. "Eh, Lord, what children go'n be saying next?"

The lady 'cross from us bust out laughing.

"That's a good one," she says. "The wind is pink. Yes sir, that's a good one."

"Don't you believe the wind is pink?" the boys says. He keeps his head down in the book.

"Course I believe it, honey," the lady says. "Course I do." She looks at us and winks her eye. "And what color is grass, honey?"

"Grass? Grass is black."

She bust out laughing again. The boy looks at her.

"Don't you believe grass is black?" he says.

The lady quits her laughing and looks at him. Everybody else looking at him, too. The place quiet, quiet.

"Grass is green, honey," the lady says. "It was green yesterday, it's green today, and it's go'n be green tomorrow."

"How do you know it's green?"

"I know because I know."

"You don't know it's green," the boy says. "You believe it's green because someone told you it was green. If someone had told you it was black you'd believe it was black."

"It's green," the lady says. "I know green when I see green."

"Prove it's green," the boy says.

"Sure, now," the lady says. "Don't tell me it's coming to that."

"It's coming to just that," the boy says. "Words mean nothing. One means no more than the other."

"That's what it all coming to?" that old lady says. That old lady got on a turban and she got on two sweaters. She got a green sweater under a black sweater. I can see the green sweater 'cause some of the buttons on the other sweater's missing.

"Yes ma'am," the boy says. "Words mean nothing. Action is the only thing. Doing. That's the only thing."

"Other words, you want the Lord to come down here and show Hisself to you?" she says.

"Exactly, ma'am," he says.

"You don't mean that, I'm sure?" she says.

"I do, ma'am," he says.

"Done, Jesus," the old lady says, shaking her head.

"I didn't go 'long with that preacher at first," the other lady says; "but now—I don't know. When a person say the grass is black, he's either a lunatic or something's wrong."

"Prove to me that it's green," the boy says.

"It's green because the people say it's green."

"Those same people say we're citizens of these United States," the boy says.

"I think I'm a citizen," the lady says.

"Citizens have certain rights," the boy says. "Name me one right that you have. One right, granted by the Constitution, that you can exercise in Bayonne."

The lady don't answer him. She just looks at him like she don't know what he's talking 'bout. I know I don't.

"Things changing," she says.

"Things are changing because some black men have begun to think with their brains and not their hearts," the boy says.

"You trying to say these people don't believe in God?"

"I'm sure some of them do. Maybe most of them do. But they don't believe that God is going to touch these white people's hearts and change things tomorrow. Things change through action. By no other way."

Everybody sit quiet and look at the boy. Nobody says a thing. Then the lady 'cross the room from me and Mama just shakes her head.

"Let's hope that not all your generation feel the same way you do," she says.

"Think what you please, it doesn't matter," the boy says. "But it will be men who listen to their heads and not their hearts who will see that your children have a better chance than you had."

"Let's hope they ain't all like you, though," the old lady says. "Done forgot the heart absolutely."

"Yes ma'am, I hope they aren't all like me," the boy says. "Unfortunately, I was born too late to believe in your God. Let's hope that the ones who come after will have your faith— if not in your God, then in something else, something definitely that they can lean on. I haven't anything. For me, the wind is pink, the grass is black."

9: The nurse comes in the room where we all sitting and waiting and says the doctor won't take no more patients till one o'clock this evening. My mama jumps up off the bench and goes up to the white lady.

"Nurse, I have to go back in the field this evening," she says.

"The doctor is treating his last patient now," the nurse says. "One o'clock this evening."

"Can I at least speak to the doctor?" my mama asks.

"I'm his nurse," the lady says.

"My little boy's sick," my mama says. "Right now his tooth almost killing him."

The nurse looks at me. She's trying to make up her mind if to let me come in. I look at her real pitiful. The tooth ain't hurting me at all, but Mama say it is, so I make 'tend for her sake.

"This evening," the nurse says, and goes on back in the office.

"Don't feel 'jected, honey," the lady says to Mama. "I been round them a long time—they take you when they want to. If you was white, that's something else; but we the wrong color."

Mama don't say nothing to the lady, and me and her go outside and stand 'gainst the wall. It's cold out there. I can feel that wind going through my coat. Some of the other people come out of the room and go up the street. Me and Mama stand there a little while and we start walking. I don't know where we going. When we come to the other street we just stand there.

"You don't have to make water, do you?" Mama says.

"No, ma'am," I say.

We go on up the street. Walking real slow. I can tell Mama don't know where she's going. When we come to a store we stand there and look at the dummies. I look at a little boy wearing a brown overcoat. He's got on brown shoes, too. I look at my old shoes and look at his'n again. You wait till summer, I say.

Me and Mama walk away. We come up to another store and we stop and look at them dummies, too. Then we go on again. We pass a café where the white people in there eating.

Mama tells me keep my eyes in front where they belong, but I can't help from seeing them people eat. My stomach starts to growling 'cause I'm hungry. When I see people eating, I get hungry; when I see a coat, I get cold.

A man whistles at my mama when we go by a filling station. She makes 'tend she don't even see him. I look back and I feel like hitting him in the mouth. If I was bigger, I say; if I was bigger, you'd see.

We keep on going. I'm getting colder and colder, but I don't say nothing. I feel that stuff running down my nose and I sniff.

"That rag," Mama says.

I get it out and wipe my nose. I'm getting cold all over now—my face, my hands, my feet, everything. We pass another little café, but this'n for white people, too, and we can't go in there, either. So we just walk. I'm so cold now I'm 'bout ready to say it. If I knowed where we was going I wouldn't be so cold, but I don't know where we going. We go, we go, we go. We walk clean out of Bayonne. Then we cross the street and we come back. Same thing I seen when I got off the bus this morning. Same old trees, same old walk, same old weeds, same old cracked pave—same old everything.

I sniff again.

"That rag," Mama says.

I wipe my nose real fast and jugg that handkerchief back in my pocket 'fore my hand gets too cold. I raise my head and I can see David's hardware store. When we come up to it, we go in. I don't know why, but I'm glad.

It's warm in there. It's so warm in there you don't ever want to leave. I look for the heater, and I see it over by them barrels. Three white men standing round the heater talking in Creole. One of them comes over to see what my mama want.

"Got any axe handles?" she says.

Me, Mama and the white man start to the back, but

Mama stops me when we come up to the heater. She and the white man go on. I hold my hands over the heater and look at them. They go all the way to the back, and I see the white man pointing to the axe handles 'gainst the wall. Mama takes one of them and shakes it like she's trying to figure how much it weighs. Then she rubs her hand over it from one end to the other end. She turns it over and looks at the other side, then she shakes it again, and shakes her head and puts it back. She gets another one and she does it just like she did the first one, then she shakes her head. Then she gets a brown one and do it that, too. But she don't like this one, either. Then she gets another one, but 'fore she shakes it or anything, she looks at me. Look like she's trying to say something to me, but I don't know what it is. All I know is I done got warm now and I'm feeling right smart better. Mama shakes this axe handle just like she did the others, and shakes her head and says something to the white man. The white man just looks at his pile of axe handles, and when Mama pass him to come to the front, the white man just scratch his head and follows her. She tells me come on and we go on out and start walking again.

We walk and walk, and no time at all I'm cold again. Look like I'm colder now 'cause I can still remember how good it was back there. My stomach growls and I suck it in to keep Mama from hearing it. She's walking right 'side me, and it growls so loud you can hear it a mile. But Mama don't say a word.

10: When we come up to the courthouse, I look at the clock. It's got quarter to twelve. Mean we got another hour and a quarter to be out here in the cold. We go and stand 'side a building. Something hits my cap and I look up at the sky. Sleet's falling.

I look at Mama standing there. I want stand close 'side

her, but she don't like that. She say that's crybaby stuff. She say you got to stand for yourself, by yourself.

"Let's go back to that office," she says.

We cross the street. When we get to the dentist office I try to open the door, but I can't. I twist and twist, but I can't. Mama pushes me to the side and she twist the knob, but she can't open the door, either. She turns 'way from the door. I look at her, but I don't move and I don't say nothing. I done seen her like this before and I'm scared of her.

"You hungry?" she says. She says it like she's mad at me, like I'm the cause of everything.

"No, ma'am," I say.

"You want eat and walk back, or you rather don't eat and ride?"

"I ain't hungry," I say.

I ain't just hungry, but I'm cold, too. I'm so hungry and cold I want to cry. And look like I'm getting colder and colder. My feet done got numb. I try to work my toes, but I don't even feel them. Look like I'm go'n die. Look like I'm go'n stand right here and freeze to death. I think 'bout home. I think 'bout Val and Auntie and Ty and Louis and Walker. It's 'bout twelve o'clock and I know they eating dinner now. I can hear Ty making jokes. He done forgot 'bout getting up early this morning and right now he's probably making jokes. Always trying to make somebody laugh. I wish I was right there listening to him. Give anything in the world if I was home round the fire.

"Come on," Mama says.

We start walking again. My feet so numb I can't hardly feel them. We turn the corner and go on back up the street. The clock on the courthouse starts hitting for twelve.

The sleet's coming down plenty now. They hit the pave and bounce like rice. Oh, Lord; oh, Lord, I pray. Don't let me die, don't let me die, don't let me die, Lord.

11: Now I know where we going. We going back of town where the colored people eat. I don't care if I don't eat. I been hungry before. I can stand it. But I can't stand the cold.

I can see we go'n have a long walk. It's 'bout a mile down there. But I don't mind. I know when I get there I'm go'n warm myself. I think I can hold out. My hands numb in my pockets and my feet numb, too, but if I keep moving I can hold out. Just don't stop no more, that's all.

The sky's gray. The sleet keeps on falling. Falling like rain now—plenty, plenty. You can hear it hitting the pave. You can see it bouncing. Sometimes it bounces two times 'fore it settles.

We keep on going. We don't say nothing. We just keep on going, keep on going.

I wonder what Mama's thinking. I hope she ain't mad at me. When summer come I'm go'n pick plenty cotton and get her a coat. I'm go'n get her a red one.

I hope they'd make it summer all the time. I'd be glad if it was summer all the time—but it ain't. We got to have winter, too. Lord, I hate the winter. I guess everybody hate the winter.

I don't sniff this time. I get out my handkerchief and wipe my nose. My hands's so cold I can hardly hold the hand-kerchief.

I think we getting close, but we ain't there yet. I wonder where everybody is. Can't see a soul but us. Look like we the only two people moving round today. Must be too cold for the rest of the people to move round in.

I can hear my teeth. I hope they don't knock together too hard and make that bad one hurt. Lord, that's all I need, for that bad one to start off.

I hear a church bell somewhere. But today ain't Sunday. They must be ringing for a funeral or something.

I wonder what they doing at home. They must be eating. Monsieur Bayonne might be there with his guitar. One day Ty played with Monsieur Bayonne's guitar and broke one of the strings. Monsieur Bayonne was some mad with Ty. He say Ty wasn't go'n ever 'mount to nothing. Ty can go just like Monsieur Bayonne when he ain't there. Ty can make everybody laugh when he starts to mocking Monsieur Bayonne.

I used to like to be with Mama and Daddy. We used to be happy. But they took him in the Army. Now, nobody happy no more. . . . I be glad when Daddy comes home.

Monsieur Bayonne say it wasn't fair for them to take Daddy and give Mama nothing and give us nothing. Auntie say, "Shhh, Etienne. Don't let them hear you talk like that." Monsieur Bayonne say, "It's God truth. What they giving his children? They have to walk three and a half miles to school hot or cold. That's anything to give for a paw? She's got to work in the field rain or shine just to make ends meet. That's anything to give for a husband?" Auntie say, "Shhh, Etienne, shhh." "Yes, you right," Monsieur Bayonne say. "Best don't say it in front of them now. But one day they go'n find out. One day." "Yes, I suppose so," Auntie say. "Then what, Rose Mary?" Monsieur Bayonne say. "I don't know, Etienne," Auntie say. "All we can do is us job, and leave everything else in His hand . . ."

We getting closer, now. We getting closer. I can even see the railroad tracks.

We cross the tracks, and now I see the café. Just to get in there, I say. Just to get in there. Already I'm starting to feel little better.

12: We go in. Ahh, it's good. I look for the heater; there 'gainst the wall. One of them little brown ones. I just stand there and hold my hands over it. I can't open my hands too wide 'cause they almost froze.

Mama's standing right 'side me. She done unbuttoned her coat. Smoke rises out of the coat, and the coat smells like a wet dog.

I move to the side so Mama can have more room. She opens out her hands and rubs them together. I rub mine together, too, 'cause this keep them from hurting. If you let them warm too fast, they hurt you sure. But if you let them warm just little bit at a time, and you keep rubbing them, they be all right every time.

They got just two more people in the café. A lady back of the counter, and a man on this side the counter. They been watching us ever since we come in.

Mama gets out the handkerchief and count up the money. Both of us know how much money she's got there. Three dollars. No, she ain't got three dollars, 'cause she had to pay us way up here. She ain't got but two dollars and a half left. Dollar and a half to get my tooth pulled, and fifty cents for us to go back on, and fifty cents worth of salt meat.

She stirs the money round with her finger. Most of the money is change 'cause I can hear it rubbing together. She stirs it and stirs it. Then she looks at the door. It's still sleeting. I can hear it hitting 'gainst the wall like rice.

"I ain't hungry, Mama," I say.

"Got to pay them something for they heat," she says.

She takes a quarter out the handkerchief and ties the handkerchief up again. She looks over her shoulder at the people, but she still don't move. I hope she don't spend the money. I don't want her spending it on me. I'm hungry, I'm almost starving I'm so hungry, but I don't want her spending the money on me.

She flips the quarter over like she's thinking. She's must be thinking 'bout us walking back home. Lord, I sure don't want walk home. If I thought it'd do any good to say something, I'd say it. But Mama makes up her own mind 'bout things.

She turns 'way from the heater right fast, like she better hurry up and spend the quarter 'fore she change her mind. I watch her go toward the counter. The man and the lady look at her, too. She tells the lady something and the lady walks away. The man keeps on looking at her. Her back's turned to the man, and she don't even know he's standing there.

The lady puts some cakes and a glass of milk on the counter. Then she pours up a cup of coffee and sets it 'side the other stuff. Mama pays her for the things and comes on back where I'm standing. She tells me sit down at the table 'gainst the wall.

The milk and the cakes's for me; the coffee's for Mama. I eat slow and I look at her. She's looking outside at the sleet. She's looking real sad. I say to myself, I'm go'n make all this up one day. You see, one day, I'm go'n make all this up. I want say it now; I want tell her how I feel right now; but Mama don't like for us to talk like that.

"I can't eat all this," I say.

They ain't got but just three little old cakes there. I'm so hungry right now, the Lord knows I can eat a hundred times three, but I want my mama to have one.

Mama don't even look my way. She knows I'm hungry, she knows I want it. I let it stay there a little while, then I get it and eat it. I eat just on my front teeth, though, 'cause if cake touch that back tooth I know what'll happen. Thank God it ain't hurt me at all today.

After I finish eating I see the man go to the juke box. He

drops a nickel in it, then he just stand there a little while looking at the record. Mama tells me keep my eyes in front where they belong. I turn my head like she say, but then I hear the man coming toward us.

"Dance, pretty?" he says.

Mama gets up to dance with him. But 'fore you know it, she done grabbed the little man in the collar and done heaved him 'side the wall. He hit the wall so hard he stop the juke box from playing.

"Some pimp," the lady back of the counter says. "Some pimp."

The little man jumps up off the floor and starts toward my mama. 'Fore you know it, Mama done sprung open her knife and she's waiting for him.

"Come on," she says. "Come on. I'll gut you from your neighbo to your throat. Come on."

I go up to the little man to hit him, but Mama makes me come and stand 'side her. The little man looks at me and Mama and goes on back to the counter.

"Some pimp," the lady back of the counter says. "Some pimp." She starts laughing and pointing at the little man. "Yes sir, you a pimp, all right. Yes sir-ree."

13: "Fasten that coat, let's go," Mama says.

"You don't have to leave," the lady says.

Mama don't answer the lady, and we right out in the cold again. I'm warm right now—my hands, my ears, my feet—but I know this ain't go'n last too long. It done sleet so much now you got ice everywhere you look.

We cross the railroad tracks, and soon's we do, I get cold. That wind goes through this little old coat like it ain't even there. I got on a shirt and a sweater under the coat, but that wind don't pay them no mind. I look up and I can see we got a long way to go. I wonder if we go'n make it 'fore I get too cold.

We cross over to walk on the sidewalk. They got just one sidewalk back here, and it's over there.

After we go just a little piece, I smell bread cooking. I look, then I see a baker shop. When we get closer, I can smell it more better. I shut my eyes and make 'tend I'm eating. But I keep them shut too long and I butt up 'gainst a telephone post. Mama grabs me and see if I'm hurt. I ain't bleeding or nothing and she turns me loose.

I can feel I'm getting colder and colder, and I look up to see how far we still got to go. Uptown is 'way up yonder. A half mile more, I reckon. I try to think of something. They say think and you won't get cold. I think of that poem, "Annabel Lee." I ain't been to school in so long—this bad weather—I reckon they done passed "Annabel Lee" by now. But passed it or not, I'm sure Miss Walker go'n make me recite it when I get there. That woman don't never forget nothing. I ain't never seen nobody like that in my life.

I'm still getting cold. "Annabel Lee" or no "Annabel Lee," I'm still getting cold. But I can see we getting closer. We getting there gradually.

Soon 's we turn the corner, I see a little old white lady up in front of us. She's the only lady on the street. She's all in black and she's got a long black rag over her head.

"Stop," she says.

Me and Mama stop and look at her. She must be crazy to be out in all this bad weather. Ain't got but a few other people out there, and all of them's men.

"Y'all done ate?" she says.

"Just finish," Mama says.

"Y'all must be cold then?" she says.

"We headed for the dentist," Mama says. "We'll warm up when we get there."

"What dentist?" the old lady says. "Mr. Bassett?"

"Yes, ma'am," Mama says.

"Come on in," the old lady says. "I'll telephone him and tell him y'all coming."

Me and Mama follow the old lady in the store. It's a little bitty store, and it don't have much in there. The old lady takes off her head rag and folds it up.

"Helena?" somebody calls from the back.

"Yes, Alnest?" the old lady says.

"Did you see them?"

"They're here. Standing beside me."

"Good. Now you can stay inside."

The old lady looks at Mama. Mama's waiting to hear what she brought us in here for. I'm waiting for that, too.

"I saw y'all each time you went by," she says. "I came out to catch you, but you were gone."

"We went back of town," Mama says.

"Did you eat?"

"Yes, ma'am."

The old lady looks at Mama a long time, like she's thinking Mama might be just saying that. Mama looks right back at her. The old lady looks at me to see what I have to say. I don't say nothing. I sure ain't going 'gainst my mama.

"There's food in the kitchen," she says to Mama. "I've been keeping it warm."

Mama turns right around and starts for the door.

"Just a minute," the old lady says. Mama stops. "The boy'll have to work for it. It isn't free."

"We don't take no handout," Mama says.

"I'm not handing out anything," the old lady says. "I need my garbage moved to the front. Ernest has a bad cold and can't go out there."

"James'll move it for you," Mama says.

"Not unless you eat," the old lady says. "I'm old, but I have my pride, too, you know."

Mama can see she ain't go'n beat this old lady down, so she just shakes her head.

"All right," the old lady says. "Come into the kitchen."

She leads the way with that rag in her hand. The kitchen is a little bitty little old thing, too. The table and the stove just 'bout fill it up. They got a little room to the side. Somebody in there laying 'cross the bed—'cause I can see one of his feet. Must be the person she was talking to: Ernest or Alnest —something like that.

"Sit down," the old lady says to Mama. "Not you," she says to me. "You have to move the cans."

"Helena?" the man says in the other room.

"Yes, Alnest?" the old lady says.

"Are you going out there again?"

"I must show the boy where the garbage is, Alnest," the old lady says.

"Keep that shawl over your head," the old man says.

"You don't have to remind me, Alnest. Come, boy," the old lady says.

We go out in the yard. Little old back yard ain't no bigger than the store or the kitchen. But it can sleet here just like it can sleet in any big back yard. And 'fore you know it, I'm trembling.

"There," the old lady says, pointing to the cans. I pick up one of the cans and set it right back down. The can's so light, I'm go'n see what's inside of it.

"Here," the old lady says. "Leave that can alone."

I look back at her standing there in the door. She's got that black rag wrapped round her shoulders, and she's pointing one of her little old fingers at me.

"Pick it up and carry it to the front," she says. I go by her with the can, and she's looking at me all the time. I'm sure the can's empty. I'm sure she could've carried it herself— maybe both of them at the same time. "Set it on the sidewalk by the door and come back for the other one," she says.

I go and come back, and Mama looks at me when I pass her. I get the other can and take it to the front. It don't feel a bit heavier than that first one. I tell myself I ain't go'n be nobody's fool, and I'm go'n look inside this can to see just what I been hauling. First, I look up the street, then down the street. Nobody coming. Then I look over my shoulder toward the door. That little old lady done slipped up there quiet 's mouse, watching me again. Look like she knowed what I was go'n do.

"Ehh, Lord," she says. "Children, children. Come in here, boy, and go wash your hands."

I follow her in the kitchen. She points toward the bathroom, and I go in there and wash up. Little bitty old bathroom, but it's clean, clean. I don't use any of her towels; I wipe my hands on my pants legs.

When I come back in the kitchen, the old lady done dished up the food. Rice, gravy, meat—and she even got some lettuce and tomato in a saucer. She even got a glass of milk and a piece of cake there, too. It looks so good, I almost start eating 'fore I say my blessing.

"Helena?" the old man says.

"Yes, Alnest?"

"Are they eating?"

"Yes," she says.

"Good," he says. "Now you'll stay inside."

The old lady goes in there where he is and I can hear them talking. I look at Mama. She's eating slow like she's thinking. I wonder what's the matter now. I reckon she's thinking 'bout home.

The old lady comes back in the kitchen.

"I talked to Dr. Bassett's nurse," she says. "Dr. Bassett will take you as soon as you get there."

"Thank you, ma'am," Mama says.

"Perfectly all right," the old lady says. "Which one is it?"

Mama nods toward me. The old lady looks at me real sad. I look sad, too.

"You're not afraid, are you?" she says.

"No, ma'am," I say.

"That's a good boy," the old lady says. "Nothing to be afraid of. Dr. Bassett will not hurt you."

When me and Mama get through eating, we thank the old lady again.

"Helena, are they leaving?" the old man says.

"Yes, Alnest."

"Tell them I say good-bye."

"They can hear you, Alnest."

"Good-bye both mother and son," the old man says. "And may God be with you."

Me and Mama tell the old man good-bye, and we follow the old lady in the front room. Mama opens the door to go out, but she stops and comes back in the store.

"You sell salt meat?" she says.

"Yes."

"Give me two bits worth."

"That isn't very much salt meat," the old lady says.

"That's all I have," Mama says.

The old lady goes back of the counter and cuts a big piece off the chunk. Then she wraps it up and puts it in a paper bag.

"Two bits," she says.

"That looks like awful lot of meat for a quarter," Mama says.

"Two bits," the old lady says. "I've been selling salt meat behind this counter twenty-five years. I think I know what I'm doing."

"You got a scale there," Mama says.

"What?" the old lady says.

"Weigh it," Mama says.

"What?" the old lady says. "Are you telling me how to run my business?"

"Thanks very much for the food," Mama says.

"Just a minute," the old lady says.

"James," Mama says to me. I move toward the door.

"Just one minute, I said," the old lady says.

Me and Mama stop again and look at her. The old lady takes the meat out of the bag and unwraps it and cuts 'bout half of it off. Then she wraps it up again and juggs it back in the bag and gives the bag to Mama. Mama lays the quarter on the counter.

"Your kindness will never be forgotten," she says. "James," she says to me.

We go out, and the old lady comes to the door to look at us. After we go a little piece I look back, and she's still there watching us.

The sleet's coming down heavy, heavy now, and I turn up my coat collar to keep my neck warm. My mama tells me turn it right back down.

"You not a bum," she says. "You a man."

Three Men

THREE MEN

Two of them was sitting in the office when I came in there. One was sitting in a chair behind the desk, the other one was sitting on the end of the desk. They looked at me, but when they saw I was just a nigger they went back to talking like I wasn't even there. They talked like that two or three more minutes before the one behind the desk looked at me again. That was T. J. I didn't know who the other one was.

"Yeah, what you want?" T. J. said.

They sat inside a little railed-in office. I went closer to the gate. It was one of them little gates that swung in and out.

"I come to turn myself in," I said.

"Turn yourself in for what?"

"I had a fight with somebody. I think I hurt him."

T. J. and the other policeman looked at me like I was crazy. I guess they had never heard of a nigger doing that before.

"You Procter Lewis?" T. J. said.

"Yes, sir."

"Come in here."

I pushed the little gate open and went in. I made sure it didn't swing back too hard and make noise. I stopped a little way from the desk. T. J. and the other policeman was watching me all the time.

"Give me some papers," T. J. said. He was looking up at me like he was still trying to figure out if I was crazy. If I wasn't crazy, then I was a smart aleck.

I got my wallet out my pocket. I could feel T. J. and the other policeman looking at me all the time. I wasn't supposed to get any papers out, myself, I was supposed to give him the wallet and let him take what he wanted. I held the wallet out to him and he jerked it out of my hand. Then he started going through everything I had in there, the money and all. After he looked at everything, he handed them to the other policeman. The other one looked at them, too; then he laid them on the desk. T. J. picked up the phone and started talking to somebody. All the time he was talking to the other person, he was looking up at me. He had a hard time making the other person believe I had turned myself in. When he hung up the phone, he told the policeman on the desk to get my records. He called the other policeman "Paul." Paul slid away from the desk and went to the file cabinet against the wall. T. J. still looked at me. His eyes was the color of ashes. I looked down at the floor, but I could still feel him looking at me. Paul came back with the records and handed them to him. I looked up again and saw them looking over the records together. Paul was standing behind T. J., looking over his shoulder.

"So you think you hurt him, huh?" T. J. asked, looking up at me again.

I didn't say anything to him. He was a mean, evil sonofabitch. He was big and red and he didn't waste time kicking your ass if you gived him the wrong answers. You had to weigh every word he said to you. Sometimes you answered, other times you kept your mouth shut. This time I passed my tongue over my lips and kept quiet.

It was about four o'clock in the morning, but it must've been seventy-five in there. T. J. and the other policeman had on short-sleeve khaki shirts. I had on a white shirt, but it was all dirty and torn. My sleeves was rolled up to the elbows, and both of my elbows was skinned and bruised.

"Didn't I bring you in here one time, myself?" Paul said.

"Yes, sir, once, I think," I said. I had been there two or three times, but I wasn't go'n say it if he didn't. I had been in couple other jails two or three times, too, but I wasn't go'n say anything about them either. If they hadn't put it on my record that was they hard luck.

"A fist fight," Paul said. "Pretty good with your fists, ain't you?"

"I protect myself," I said.

It was quiet in there for a second or two. I knowed why; I hadn't answered the right way.

"You protect yourself, what?" T. J. said.

"I protect myself, *sir*," I said.

They still looked at me. But I could tell Paul wasn't anything like T. J. He wasn't mean at all, he just had to play mean because T. J. was there. Couple Sundays ago I had played baseball with a boy who looked just like Paul. But he had brown eyes; Paul had blue eyes.

"You'll be sorry you didn't use your fists this time," T. J. said. "Take everything out your pockets."

I did what he said.

"Where's your knife?" he asked.

"I never car' a knife," I said.

"You never car' a knife, what, boy?" T. J. said.

"I never car' a knife, *sir*," I said.

He looked at me hard again. He didn't think I was crazy for turning myself in, he thought I was a smart aleck. I could tell from his big, fat, red face he wanted to hit me with his fist.

He nodded to Paul and Paul came toward me. I moved back some.

"I'm not going to hurt you," Paul said.

I stopped, but I could still feel myself shaking. Paul started patting me down. He found a pack of cigarettes in my shirt pocket. I could see in his face he didn't want take them out, but he took them out, anyhow.

"Thought I told you empty your pockets?" T. J. said.

"I didn't know—"

"Paul, if you can't make that boy shut up, I can," T. J. said.

"He'll be quiet," Paul said, looking at me. He was telling me with his eyes to be quiet or I was go'n get myself in a lot of trouble.

"You got one more time to butt in," T. J. said. "One more time now."

I was getting a swimming in the head, and I looked down at the floor. I hoped they would hurry up and lock me up so I could have a little peace.

"Why'd you turn yourself in?" T. J. asked.

I kept my head down. I didn't answer him.

"Paul, can't you make that boy talk?" T. J. said. "Or do I have to get up and do it?"

"He'll talk," Paul said.

"I figured y'all was go'n catch me sooner or later—sir."

"That's not the reason you turned yourself in," T. J. said.

I kept my head down.

"Look up when I talk to you," T. J. said.

I raised my head. I felt weak and shaky. My clothes was wet and sticking to my body, but my mouth felt dry as dust. My eyes wanted to look down again, but I forced myself to look at T. J.'s big red face.

"You figured if you turned yourself in, Roger Medlow was go'n get you out, now, didn't you?"

I didn't say anything—but that's exactly what I was figuring on.

"Sure," he said. He looked at me a long time. He knowed how I was feeling; he knowed I was weak and almost ready to fall. That's why he was making me stand there like that. "What you think we ought to do with niggers like you?" he said. "Come on now—what you think we ought to do with you?"

I didn't answer him.

"Well?" he said.

"I don't know," I said. "Sir."

"I'll tell you," he said. "See, if I was gov'nor, I'd run every damned one of you off in that river out there. Man, woman and child. You know that?"

I was quiet, looking at him. But I made sure I didn't show in my face what I was thinking. I could've been killed for what I was thinking then.

"Well, what you think of that?" he said.

"That's up to the gov'nor, sir," I said.

"Yeah," he said. "That's right. That's right. I think I'll write him a little telegram and tell him 'bout my idea. Can save this state a hell of a lot trouble."

Now he just sat there looking at me again. He wanted to hit me in the mouth with his fist. Not just hit me, he wanted to beat me. But he had to have a good excuse. And what excuse could he have when I had already turned myself in.

"Put him in there with Munford," he said to Paul.

We went out. We had to walk down a hall to the cell block. The niggers' cell block was on the second floor. We had to go up some concrete steps to get there. Paul turned on the lights and a woman hollered at him to turn them off. "What's this supposed to be—Christmas?" she said. "A person can't sleep in this joint." The women was locked up on one end of the block and the men was at the other end. If you had a mirror or a piece of shiny tin, you could stick it out the cell and fix it so you could see the other end of the block.

The guard opened the cell door and let me in, then he locked it back. I looked at him through the bars.

"When will y'all ever learn?" he said, shaking his head.

He said it like he meant it, like he was sorry for me. He kept reminding me of that boy I had played baseball with. They called that other boy Lloyd, and he used to show up just about every Sunday to play baseball with us. He used to play the outfield so he could do a lot of running. He used to buy Cokes for everybody after the game. He was the only white boy out there.

"Here's a pack of cigarettes and some matches," Paul said. "Might not be your brand, but I doubt if you'll mind it too much in there."

I took the cigarettes from him.

"You can say 'Thanks,' " he said.

"Thanks," I said.

"And you can say 'sir' sometimes," he said.

"Sir," I said.

He looked at me like he felt sorry for me, like he felt sorry for everybody. He didn't look like a policeman at all.

"Let me give you a word of warning," he said. "Don't push T. J. Don't push him, now."

"I won't."

"It doesn't take much to get him started—don't push him."

I nodded.

"Y'all go'n turn out them goddamn lights?" the woman hollered from the other end of the block.

"Take it easy," Paul said to me and left.

After the lights went out, I stood at the cell door till my eyes got used to the dark. Then I climbed up on my bunk. Two other people was in the cell. Somebody on the bunk under mine, somebody on the lower bunk 'cross from me. The upper bunk 'cross from me was empty.

"Cigarette?" the person below me said.

He said it very low, but I could tell he was talking to me and not to the man 'cross from us. I shook a cigarette out the pack and dropped it on the bunk. I could hear the man scratching the match to light the cigarette. He cupped his hands close to his face, because I didn't see too much light. I could tell from the way he let that smoke out he had wanted a cigarette very bad.

"What you in for?" he said, real quiet.

"A fight," I said.

"First time?"

"No, I been in before."

He didn't say any more and I didn't, either. I didn't feel like talking, anyhow. I looked up at the window on my left, and I could see a few stars. I felt lonely and I felt like crying. But I couldn't cry. Once you started that in here you was done for. Everybody and his brother would run over you.

The man on the other bunk got up to take a leak. The toilet was up by the head of my bunk. After the man had zipped up his pants, he just stood there looking at me. I tightened my fist to swing at him if he tried any funny stuff.

"Well, hello there," he said.

"Get your ass back over there, Hattie," the man below me said. He spoke in that quiet voice again. "Hattie is a woman," he said to me. "Don't see how come they didn't put him with the rest of them whores."

"Don't let it worry your mind," Hattie said.

"Caught him playing with this man dick," the man below me said. "At this old flea-bitten show back of town there. Up front—front row—there he is playing with this man dick. Bitch."

"Is that any worse than choking somebody half to death?" Hattie said.

The man below me was quiet. Hattie went back to his bunk.

"Oh, these old crampy, stuffy, old ill-smelling beds," he said, slapping the mattress level with the palm of his hand. "How do they expect you to sleep." He laid down. "What are you in for, honey?" he asked me. "You look awful young."

"Fighting," I said.

"You poor, poor thing," Hattie said. "If I can help you in any way, don't hesitate to ask."

"Shit," the man below me said. I heard him turning over so he could go to sleep.

"The world has given up on the likes of you," Hattie said. "You jungle beast."

"Bitch, why don't you just shut up," the man said.

"Why don't both of y'all shut up," somebody said from another cell.

It was quiet after that.

I looked up at the window and I could see the stars going out in the sky. My eyes felt tired and my head started spinning, and I wasn't here any more, I was at the Seven Spots. And she was there in red, and she had two big dimples in her jaws. Then she got up and danced with him, and every time she turned my way she looked over his shoulder at me and smiled. And when she turned her back to me, she rolled her big ass real slow and easy—just for me, just for me. Grinning Boy was sitting at the table with me, saying: "Poison, poison—nothing but poison. Look at that; just look at that." I was looking, but I wasn't thinking about what he was saying. When she went back to that table to sit down, I went there and asked her to dance. That nigger sitting there just looked at me, rolling his big white eyes like I was supposed to break out of the joint. I didn't pay him no mind, I was looking at that woman. And I was looking down at them two big pretty brown things poking that dress way out. They looked so soft and warm and waiting, I wanted to touch them right there in front of that ugly nigger. She shook her head, because he was sitting there, but little bit later when she went back in the kitchen, I went back there, too. Grinning Boy tried to stop me, saying, "Poison, poison, poison," but I didn't pay him no mind. When I came back in the kitchen, she was standing at the counter ordering a chicken sandwich. The lady back of the counter had to fry the chicken, so she had to wait a while. When she saw me, she started smiling. Them two big dimples came in her jaws. I smiled back at her.

"She go'n take a while," I said. "Let's step out in the cool till she get done."

She looked over her shoulder and didn't see the nigger peeping, and we went outside. There was people talking out there, but I didn't care, I had to touch her.

"What's your name?" I said.

"Clara."

"Let's go somewhere, Clara."

"I can't. I'm with somebody," she said.

"That nigger?" I said. "You call him somebody?"

She just looked at me with that little smile on her face— them two big dimples in her jaws. I looked little farther down, and I could see how them two warm, brown things was waiting for somebody to tear that dress open so they could get free.

"You must be the prettiest woman in the world," I said.

"You like me?"

"Lord, yes."

"I want you to like me," she said.

"Then what's keeping us from going?" I said. "Hell away with that nigger."

"My name is Clara Johnson," she said. "It's in the book. Call me tomorrow after four."

She turned to go back inside, but just then that big sweaty nigger bust out the door. He passed by her like she wasn't even there.

"No, Bayou," she said. "No."

But he wasn't listening to a thing. Before I knowed it, he had cracked me on the chin and I was down on my back. He raised his foot to kick me in the stomach, and I rolled and rolled till I was out of the way. Then I jumped back up.

"I don't want fight you, Bayou," I said. "I don't want fight you, now."

"You fight or you fly, nigger," somebody else said. "If you run, we go'n catch you."

Bayou didn't say nothing. He just came in swinging. I backed away from him.

"I wasn't doing nothing but talking to her," I said.

He rushed in and knocked me on a bunch of people. They picked me clear off the ground and throwed me back on him. He hit me again, this time a glancing blow on the shoulder. I moved back from him, holding the shoulder with the other hand.

"I don't want fight you," I told him. "I was just talking to her."

But trying to talk to Bayou was like trying to talk to a mule. He came in swinging wild and high, and I went under his arm and rammed my fist in his stomach. But it felt like ramming your fist into a hundred-pound sack of flour. He stopped about a half a second, then he was right back on me again. I hit him in the face this time, and I saw the blood splash out of his mouth. I was still backing away from him, hoping he would quit, but the nigger kept coming on me. He had to, because all his friends and that woman was there. But he didn't know how to fight, and every time he moved in I hit him in the face. Then I saw him going for his knife.

"Watch it, now, Bayou," I said. "I don't have a knife. Let's keep this fair."

But he didn't hear a thing I was saying; he was listening to the others who was sicking him on. He kept moving in on me. He had both of his arms 'way out—that blade in his right hand. From the way he was holding it, he didn't have nothing but killing on his mind.

I kept moving back, moving back. Then my foot touched a bottle and I stooped down and picked it up. I broke it against the corner of the building, but I never took my eyes off Bayou. He started circling me with the knife, and I moved round him with the bottle. He made a slash at me, and I jumped back. He was all opened and I could've gotten him then, but I was still hoping for him to change his mind.

"Let's stop it, Bayou," I kept saying to him. "Let's stop it, now."

But he kept on circling me with the knife, and I kept on going round him with the bottle. I didn't look at his face any more, I kept my eyes on that knife. It was a Texas jack with a pearl handle, and that blade must've been five inches long.

"Stop it, Bayou," I said. "Stop it, stop it."

He slashed at me, and I jumped back. He slashed at me again, and I jumped back again. Then he acted like a fool and ran on me, and all I did was stick the bottle out. I felt it go in his clothes and in his stomach and I felt the hot, sticky blood on my hand and I saw his face all twisted and sweaty. I felt his hands brush against mine when he throwed both of his hands up to his stomach. I started running. I was running toward the car, and Grinning Boy was running there, too. He got there before me and jumped in on the driving side, but I pushed him out the way and got under that ste'r'n' wheel. I could hear that gang coming after me, and I shot that Ford out of there a hundred miles an hour. Some of them ran up

131

the road to cut me off, but when they saw I wasn't stopping they jumped out of the way. Now, it was nobody but me, that Ford and that gravel road. Grinning Boy was sitting over there crying, but I wasn't paying him no mind. I wanted to get much road between me and Seven Spots as I could.

After I had gone a good piece, I slammed on the brakes and told Grinning Boy to get out. He wouldn't get out. I opened the door and pushed on him, but he held the ste'r'n' wheel. He was crying and holding the wheel with both hands. I hit him and pushed on him and hit him and pushed on him, but he wouldn't turn it loose. If they was go'n kill me, I didn't want them to kill him, too, but he couldn't see that. I shot away from there with the door still opened, and after we had gone a little piece, Grinning Boy reached out and got it and slammed it again.

I came out on the pave road and drove three or four miles 'long the river. Then I turned down a dirt road and parked the car under a big pecan tree. It was one of these old plantation quarter and the place was quiet as a graveyard. It was pretty bright, though, because the moon and the stars was out. The dust in that long, old road was white as snow. I lit a cigarette and tried to think. Grinning Boy was sitting over there crying. He was crying real quiet with his head hanging down on his chest. Every now and then I could hear him sniffing.

"I'm turning myself in," I said.

I had been thinking and thinking and I couldn't think of nothing else to do. I knowed Bayou was dead or hurt pretty bad, and I knowed either that gang or the law was go'n get me, anyhow. I backed the car out on the pave road and drove to Bayonne. I told Grinning Boy to let my uncle know I was in trouble. My uncle would go to Roger Medlow—and I was hoping Roger Medlow would get me off like he had done once before. He owned the plantation where I lived.

"Hey," somebody was calling and shaking me. "Hey, there, now; wake up."

I opened my eyes and looked at this old man standing by the head of my bunk. I'm sure if I had woke up anywhere else and found him that close to me I would've jumped back screaming. He must've been sixty; he had reddish-brown eyes, and a stubby gray beard. 'Cross his right jaw, from his cheekbone to his mouth, was a big shiny scar where somebody had gotten him with a razor. He was wearing a derby hat, and he had it cocked a little to the back of his head.

"They coming," he said.

"Who?"

"Breakfast."

"I'm not hungry."

"You better eat. Never can tell when you go'n eat again in this joint."

His breath didn't smell too good either, and he was standing so close to me, I could smell his breath every time he breathed in and out. I figured he was the one they called Munford. Just before they brought me down here last night, I heard T. J. tell Paul to put me in there with Munford. Since he had called the other one Hattie, I figured he was Munford.

"Been having yourself a nice little nightmare," he said. "Twisting and turning there like you wanted to fall off. You can have this bunk of mine tonight if you want."

I looked at the freak laying on the other bunk. He looked back at me with a sad little smile on his face.

"I'll stay here," I said.

The freak stopped smiling, but he still looked sad—like a sad woman. He knowed why I didn't want get down there. I didn't want no part of him.

Out on the cell block, the nigger trustee was singing. He went from one cell to the other one singing, "Come and get it, it's hot. What a lovely, lovely day, isn't it? Yes, indeed," he answered himself. "Yes, indeed . . . Come and get it, my children, come and get it. Unc' Toby won't feel right if y'all don't eat his lovely food."

He stopped before the cell with his little shiny pushcart. A white guard was with him. The guard opened the cell door and Unc' Toby gived each one of us a cup of coffee and two baloney sandwiches. Then the guard shut the cell again and him and Unc' Toby went on up the block. Unc' Toby was singing again.

"Toby used to have a little stand," Munford said to me. "He think he still got it. He kinda loose up here," he said, tapping his head with the hand that held the sandwiches.

"They ought to send him to Jackson if he's crazy."

"They like keeping him here," Munford said. "Part of the scheme of things."

"You want this?" I asked.

"No, eat it," he said.

I got back on my bunk. I ate one of the sandwiches and drank some of the coffee. The coffee was nothing but brown water. It didn't have any kind of taste—not even bitter taste. I drank about half and poured the rest in the toilet.

The freak, Hattie, sat on his bunk, nibbling at his food. He wrapped one slice of bread round the slice of baloney and ate that, then he did the same thing with the other sandwich. The two extra slices of bread, he dipped down in his coffee and ate it like that. All the time he was eating, he was looking at me like a sad woman looks at you.

Munford stood between the two rows of bunks, eating and drinking his coffee. He pressed both of the sandwiches together and ate them like they was just one. Nobody said anything all the time we was eating. Even when I poured out the coffee, nobody said anything. The freak just looked at me like a sad woman. But Munford didn't look at me at all—he was looking up at the window all the time. When he got through eating, he wiped his mouth and throwed his cup on his bunk.

"Another one of them smokes," he said to me.

The way he said it, it sounded like he would've took it if I didn't give it to him. I got out the pack of cigarettes and gived him one. He lit it and took a big draw. I was laying back against the wall, looking up at the window; but I could tell that Munford was looking at me.

"Killed somebody, huh?" Munford said, in his quiet, calm voice.

"I cut him pretty bad," I said, still looking up at the window.

"He's dead," Munford said.

I wouldn't take my eyes off the window. My throat got tight, and my heart started beating so loud, I'm sure both Munford and that freak could hear it.

"That's bad," Munford said.

"And so young," Hattie said. I didn't have to look at the freak to know he was crying. "And so much of his life still before him—my Lord."

"You got people?" Munford asked.

"Uncle," I said.

"You notified him?"

"I think he knows."

"You got a lawyer?"

"No."

"No money?"

"No."

"That's bad," he said.

"Maybe his uncle can do something," Hattie said. "Poor thing." Then I heard him blowing his nose.

I looked at the bars in the window. I wanted them to leave me alone so I could think.

"So young, too," Hattie said. "My Lord, my Lord."

"Oh shut up," Munford said. "I don't know why they didn't lock you up with the rest of them whores."

"Is it too much to have some feeling of sympathy?" Hattie said, and blowed his nose again.

"Morris David is a good lawyer," Munford said. "Get him if you can. Best for colored round here."

I nodded, but I didn't look at Munford. I felt bad and I wanted them to leave me alone.

"Was he a local boy?" Munford asked.

"I don't know," I said.

"Where was it?"

I didn't answer him.

"Best to talk 'bout it," Munford said. "Keeping it in just make it worse."

"Seven Spots," I said.

"That's a rough joint," Munford said.

"They're all rough joints," Hattie said. "That's all you have—rough joints. No decent places for someone like him."

"Who's your uncle?" Munford asked.

"Martin Baptiste. Medlow plantation."

"Martin Baptiste?" Munford said.

I could tell from the way he said it, he knowed my uncle. I looked at him now. He was looking back at me with his left eye half shut. I could tell from his face he didn't like my uncle.

"You same as out already," he said.

He didn't like my uncle at all, and now he was studying me to see how much I was like him.

"Medlow can get you out of here just by snapping his fingers," he said. "Big men like that run little towns like these."

"I killed somebody," I said.

"You killed another old nigger," Munford said. "A nigger ain't nobody."

He drawed on the cigarette, and I looked at the big scar on the side of his face. He took the cigarette from his mouth and patted the scar with the tip of one of his fingers.

"Bunch of them jumped on me one night," he said. "One caught me with a straight razor. Had the flesh hanging so much, I coulda ripped it off with my hands if I wanted to. Ah, but before I went down you shoulda seen what I did the bunch of 'em." He stopped and thought a while. He even laughed a little to himself. "I been in this joint so much, everybody from the judge on down know me. 'How's it going, Munford?' 'Well, you back with us again, huh, Munt?' 'Look, y'all, old Munt's back with us again, just like he said he'd be.' They all know me. All know me. I'll get out little later on. What time is it getting to be—'leven? I'll give 'em till twelve and tell 'em I want get out. They'll let me out. Got in Saturday night. They always keep me from Saturday till Monday. If it rain, they keep me till Tuesday—don't want me get out and catch cold, you know. Next Saturday, I'm right back. Can't stay out of here to save my soul."

"Places like these are built for people like you," Hattie said. "Not for decent people."

"Been going in and out of these jails here, I don't know how long," Munford said. "Forty, fifty years. Started out just like you—kilt a boy just like you did last night. Kilt him and got off—got off scot-free. My pappy worked for a white man who got me off. At first I didn't know why he had done it—I didn't think; all I knowed was I was free, and free is how I wanted to be. Then I got in trouble again, and again they got me off. I kept on getting in trouble, and they kept on getting me off. Didn't wake up till I got to be nearly old as I'm is now. Then I realized they kept getting me off because they needed a Munford Bazille. They need me to prove they human—just like they need that thing over there. They need us. Because without us, they don't know what they is—they don't know what they is out there. With us around, they can

137

see us and they know what they ain't. They ain't us. Do you see? Do you see how they think?"

I didn't know what he was talking about. It was hot in the cell and he had started sweating. His face was wet, except for that big scar. It was just laying there smooth and shiny.

"But I got news for them. They us. I never tell them that, but inside I know it. They us, just like we is ourselves. Cut any of them open and you see if you don't find Munford Bazille or Hattie Brown there. You know what I mean?"

"I guess so."

"No, you don't know what I mean," he said. "What I mean is not one of them out there is a man. Not one. They think they men. They think they men 'cause they got me and him in here who ain't men. But I got news for them—cut them open; go 'head and cut one open—you see if you don't find Munford Bazille or Hattie Brown. Not a man one of them. 'Cause face don't make a man—black or white. Face don't make him and fucking don't make him and fighting don't make him—neither killing. None of this prove you a man. 'Cause animals can fuck, can kill, can fight—you know that?"

I looked at him, but I didn't answer him. I didn't feel like answering.

"Well?" he said.

"Yeah."

"Then answer me when I ask you a question. I don't like talking to myself."

He stopped and looked at me a while.

"You know what I'm getting at?"

"No," I said.

"To hell if you don't," he said. "Don't let Medlow get you out of here so you can kill again."

"You got out," I said.

"Yeah," he said, "and I'm still coming back here and I'm

still getting out. Next Saturday I'm go'n hit another nigger in the head, and Saturday night they go'n bring me here, and Monday they go'n let me out again. And Saturday after that I'm go'n hit me another nigger in the head—'cause I'll hit a nigger in the head quick as I'll look at one."

"You're just an animal out the black jungle," Hattie said. "Because you have to hit somebody in the head every Saturday night don't mean he has to do the same."

"He'll do it," Munford said, looking at me, not at Hattie. "He'll do it 'cause he know Medlow'll get him out. Won't you?"

I didn't answer him. Munford nodded his head.

"Yeah, he'll do it. They'll see to that."

He looked at me like he was mad at me, then he looked up at the bars in the window. He frowned and rubbed his hand over his chin, and I could hear the gritty sound his beard made. He studied the bars a long time, like he was thinking about something 'way off; then I saw how his face changed: his eyes twinkled and he grinned to himself. He turned to look at Hattie laying on the bunk.

"Look here," he said. "I got a few coppers and a few minutes—what you say me and you giving it a little whirl?"

"My God, man," Hattie said. He said it the way a young girl would've said it if you had asked her to pull down her drawers. He even opened his eyes wide the same way a young girl would've done it. "Do you think I could possibly ever sink so low?" he said.

"Well, that's what you do on the outside," Munford said.

"What I do on the outside is absolutely no concern of yours, let me assure you," the freak said. "And furthermore, I have friends that I associate with."

"And them 'sociating friends you got there—what they got Munford don't have?" Munford said.

"For one thing, manners," Hattie said. "Of all the nerve."

Munford grinned at him and looked at me.

"You know what make 'em like that?" he asked.

"No."

He nodded his head. "Then I'll tell you. It start in the cradle when they send that preacher there to christen you. At the same time he's doing that mumbo-jumbo stuff, he's low'ing his mouth to your little nipper to suck out your manhood. I know, he tried it on me. Here, I'm laying in his arms in my little white blanket and he suppose to be christening me. My mammy there, my pappy there; uncle, aunt, grandmammy, grandpappy; my nan-nane, my pa-ran—all of them standing there with they head bowed. This preacher going, 'Mumbo-jumbo, mumbo-jumbo,' but all the time he's low'ing his mouth toward my little private. Nobody else don't see him, but I catch him, and I haul 'way back and hit him right smack in the eye. I ain't no more than three months old but I give him a good one. 'Get your goddamn mouth away from my little pecker, you no-teef, rotten, egg-sucking sonofabitch. Get away from here, you sister-jumper, God-calling, pulpit-spitting, mother-huncher. Get away from here, you chicken-eating, catfish-eating, gin-drinking sonofa-bitch. Get away, goddamn it, get away . . .' "

I thought Munford was just being funny, but he was serious as he could ever get. He had worked himself up so much, he had to stop and catch his breath.

"That's what I told him," he said. "That's what I told him. . . . But they don't stop there, they stay after you. If they miss you in the cradle, they catch you some other time. And when they catch you, they draw it out of you or they make you a beast—make you use it in a brutish way. You use it on a woman without caring for her, you use it on children, you use it on other men, you use it on yourself. Then when you get so disgusted with everything round you, you kill. And if your back is strong, like your back is strong, they get you out so you can kill again." He stopped and looked at me and nodded his head. "Yeah, that's what they do with you—exactly. . . . But not everybody end up like that. Some of them make it. Not many—but some of them do make it."

"Going to the pen?" I said.

"Yeah—the pen is one way," he said. "But you don't go to the pen for the nigger you killed. Not for him—he ain't worth it. They told you that from the cradle—a nigger ain't worth a good gray mule. Don't mention a white mule: fifty niggers ain't worth a good white mule. So you don't go to the pen for killing the nigger, you go for yourself. You go to sweat out all the crud you got in your system. You go, saying, 'Go fuck yourself, Roger Medlow, I want to be a man, and by God I will be a man. For once in my life I will be a man.'"

"And a month after you been in the pen, Medlow tell them to kill you for being a smart aleck. How much of a man you is then?"

"At least you been a man a month—where if you let him get you out you won't be a man a second. He won't 'low it."

"I'll take that chance," I said.

He looked at me a long time now. His reddish-brown eyes was sad and mean. He felt sorry for me, and at the same time he wanted to hit me with his fist.

"You don't look like that whitemouth uncle of yours," he said. "And you look much brighter than I did at your age. But I guess every man must live his own life. I just wish I had mine to live all over again."

He looked up at the window like he had given up on me. After a while, he looked back at Hattie on the bunk.

"You not thinking 'bout what I asked you?" he said.

Hattie looked up at him just like a woman looks at a man she can't stand.

"Munford, if you dropped dead this second, I doubt if I would shed a tear."

"Put all that together, I take it you mean no," Munford said.

Hattie rolled his eyes at Munford the way a woman rolls her eyes at a man she can't stand.

"Well, I better get out of here," Munford said. He passed his hand over his chin. It sounded like passing your hand over sandpaper. "Go home and take me a shave and might go out and do little fishing," he said. "Too hot to pick cotton."

He looked at me again.

"I guess I'll be back next week or the week after—but I suppose you'll be gone to Medlow by then."

"If he come for me—yes."

"He'll come for you," Munford said. "How old you is—twenty?"

"Nineteen."

"Yeah, he'll come and take you back. And next year you'll kill another old nigger. 'Cause they grow niggers just to be killed, and they grow people like you to kill 'em. That's all part of the—the culture. And every man got to play his part in the culture, or the culture don't go on. But I'll tell you this; if you was kin to anybody else except that Martin Baptiste, I'd stay in here long enough to make you go to Angola. 'Cause I'd break your back 'fore I let you walk out of this cell with Medlow. But with Martin Baptiste blood in you, you'll never be worth a goddamn no matter what I did. With that, I bid you adieu."

He tipped his derby to me, then he went to the door and called for the guard. The guard came and let him out. The people on the block told him good-bye and said they would see him when they got out. Munford waved at them and followed the guard toward the door.

"That Munford," Hattie said. "Thank God we're not all

like that." He looked up at me. "I hope you didn't listen to half of that nonsense."

I didn't answer the freak—I didn't want have nothing to do with him. I looked up at the window. The sky was darkish blue and I could tell it was hot out there. I had always hated the hot sun, but I wished I was out there now. I wouldn't even mind picking cotton, much as I hated picking cotton.

I got out my other sandwich: nothing but two slices of light bread and a thin slice of baloney sausage. If I wasn't hungry, I wouldn't 'a' ate it at all. I tried to think about what everybody was doing at home. But hard as I tried, all I could think about was here. Maybe it was best if I didn't think about outside. That could run you crazy. I had heard about people going crazy in jail. I tried to remember how it was when I was in jail before. It wasn't like this if I could remember. Before, it was just a brawl—a fight. I had never stayed in more than a couple weeks. I had been in about a half dozen times, but never more than a week or two. This time it was different, though. Munford said Roger Medlow was go'n get me out, but suppose Munford was wrong. Suppose I had to go up? Suppose I had to go to the pen?

Hattie started singing. He was singing a spiritual and he was singing it in a high-pitched voice like a woman. I wanted to tell him to shut up, but I didn't want have nothing to do with that freak. I could feel him looking at me; a second later he had quit singing.

"That Munford," he said. "I hope you didn't believe everything he said about me."

I was quiet. I didn't want to talk to Hattie. He saw it and kept his mouth shut.

If Medlow was go'n get me out of here, why hadn't he done so? If all he had to do was snap his fingers, what was keeping him from snapping them? Maybe he wasn't go'n do anything for me. I wasn't one of them Uncle Tom-ing niggers like my uncle, and maybe he was go'n let me go up this time.

I couldn't make it in the pen. Locked up—caged. Walking round all day with shackles on my legs. No woman, no pussy—I'd die in there. I'd die in a year. Not five years—one year. If Roger Medlow came, I was leaving. That's how old people is: they always want you to do something they never did when they was young. If he had his life to live all over— how come he didn't do it then? Don't tell me do it when he didn't do it. If that's part of the culture, then I'm part of the culture, because I sure ain't for the pen.

That black sonofabitch—that coward. I hope he didn't have religion. I hope his ass burn in hell till eternity.

Look how life can change on you—just look. Yesterday this time I was poon-tanging like a dog. Today—that black sonofabitch—behind these bars maybe for the rest of my life. And look at me, look at me. Strong. A man. A damn good man. A hard dick—a pile of muscles. But look at me—locked in here like a caged animal.

Maybe that's what Munford was talking about. You spend much time in here like he done spent, you can't be nothing but a' animal.

I wish somebody could do something for me. I can make a phone call, can't I? But call who? That ass-hole uncle of mine? I'm sure Grinning Boy already told him where I'm at. I wonder if Grinning Boy got in touch with Marie. I suppose this finish it. Hell, why should she stick her neck out for me. I was treating her like a dog, anyhow. I'm sorry, baby; I'm sorry. No, I'm not sorry; I'd do the same thing tomorrow if I was out of here. Maybe I'm a' animal already. I don't care who she is, I'd do it with her and don't give a damn. Hell, let me stop whining; I ain't no goddamn animal. I'm a man, and I got to act and think like a man.

I got to think, I got to think. My daddy is somewhere up North—but where? I got more people scattered around, but no use going to them. I'm the black sheep of this family—and they don't care if I live or die. They'd be glad if I died so they'd be rid of me for good.

That black sonofabitch—I swear to God. Big as he was, he had to go for a knife. I hope he rot in hell. I hope he burn—goddamn it—till eternity come and go.

Let me see, let me see, who can I call? I don't know a soul with a dime. Them white people out there got it, but what do they care 'bout me, a nigger. Now, if I was a' Uncle Tom-ing nigger—oh, yes, they'd come then. They'd come running. But like I'm is, I'm fucked. Done for.

Five years, five years—that's what they give you. Five years for killing a nigger like that. Five years out of my life. Five years for a rotten, no good sonofabitch who didn't have no business being born in the first place. Five years . . .

Maybe I ought to call Medlow myself. . . . But suppose he come, then what? Me and Medlow never got along. I couldn't never bow and say, "Yes sir," and scratch my head. But I'd have to do it now. He'd have me by the nuts and he'd know it; and I'd have to kiss his ass if he told me to.

Oh Lord, have mercy. . . . They get you, don't they. They let you run and run, then they get you. They stick a no-good, trashy nigger up there, and they get you. And they twist your nuts and twist them till you don't care no more.

I got to stop this, I got to stop it. My head'll go to hurting after while and I won't be able to think anything out.

"Oh, you're so beautiful when you're meditating," Hattie said. "And what were you meditating about?"

I didn't answer him—I didn't want have nothing to do with that freak.

"How long you're going to be in here, is that it?" he said. "Sometimes they let you sit for days and days. In your case they might let you sit here a week before they say anything to you. What do they care—they're inhuman."

I got a cigarette out of the pack and lit it.

"I smoke, too," Hattie said.

I didn't answer that freak. He came over and got the pack out of my shirt pocket. His fingers went down in my pocket just like a woman's fingers go in your pocket.

"May I?" he said.

I didn't say nothing to him. He lit his cigarette and laid the pack on my chest just like a woman'd do it.

"Really, I'm not all that awful," he said. "Munford has poisoned your mind with all sorts of notions. Let go—relax. You need friends at a time like this."

I stuffed the pack of cigarettes in my pocket and looked up at the window.

"These are very good," the freak said. "Very, very good. Well, maybe you'll feel like talking a little later on. It's always good to let go. I'm understanding; I'll be here."

He went back to his bunk and laid down.

Toward three o'clock, they let the women out of the cells to walk around. Some of the women came down the block and talked to the men through the bars. Some of them even laughed and joked. Three-thirty, the guard locked them up and let the men out. From the way the guard looked at me, I knowed I wasn't going anywhere. I didn't want to go anywhere, either, because I didn't want people asking me a pile of questions. Hattie went out to stretch, but few minutes later he came and laid back down. He was grumbling about some man on the block trying to get fresh with him.

"Some of them think you'll stoop to anything," he said.

I looked out of the window at the sky. I couldn't see too much, but I liked what I could see. I liked the sun, too. I hadn't ever liked the sun before, but I liked it now. I felt my throat getting tight, and I turned my head.

Toward four o'clock, Unc' Toby came on the block with

dinner. For dinner, we had stew, mashed potatoes, lettuce and tomatoes. The stew was too soupy; the mashed potatoes was too soupy; the lettuce and tomatoes was too soggy. Dessert was three or four dried-up prunes with black water poured over them. After Unc' Toby served us, the guard locked up the cell. By the time we finished eating, they was back there again to pick up the trays.

I laid on my bunk, looking up at the window. How long I had been there? No more than about twelve hours. Twelve hours—but it felt like three days, already.

They knowed how to get a man down. Because they had me now. No matter which way I went—plantation or pen—they had me. That's why Medlow wasn't in any hurry to get me out. You don't have to be in any hurry when you already know you got a man by the nuts.

Look at the way they did Jack. Jack was a man, a good man. Look what they did him. Let a fifteen-cents Cajun bond him out of jail—a no-teeth, dirty, overall-wearing Cajun get him out. Then they broke him. Broke him down to nothing—to a grinning, bowing fool. . . . We loved Jack. Jack could do anything. Work, play ball, run women—anything. They knowed we loved him, that's why they did him that. Broke him—broke him the way you break a wild horse. . . . Now everybody laughs at him. Gamble with him and cheat him. He know you cheating him, but he don't care—just don't care any more . . .

Where is my father? Why my mama had to die? Why they brought me here and left me to struggle like this? I used to love my mama so much. Her skin was light brown; her hair was silky. I used to watch her powdering her face in the glass. I used to always cry when she went out—and be glad when she came back because she always brought me candy. But you gone for good now, Mama; and I got nothing in this world but me.

A man in the other cell started singing. I listened to him

and looked up at the window. The sky had changed some more. It was lighter blue now—gray-blue almost.

The sun went down, a star came out. For a while it was the only star; then some more came to join it. I watched all of them. Then I watched just a few, then just one. I shut my eyes and opened them and tried to find the star again. I couldn't find it. I wasn't too sure which one it was. I could've pretended and choosed either one, but I didn't want lie to myself. I don't believe in lying to myself. I don't believe in lying to nobody else, either. I believe in being straight with a man. And I want a man to be straight with me. I wouldn't 'a' picked up that bottle for nothing if that nigger hadn't pulled his knife. Not for nothing. Because I don't believe in that kind of stuff. I believe in straight stuff. But a man got to protect himself . . . But with stars I wasn't go'n cheat. If I didn't know where the one was I was looking at at first, I wasn't go'n say I did. I picked out another one, one that wasn't too much in a cluster. I measured it off from the bars in the window, then I shut my eyes. When I opened them, I found the star right away. And I didn't have to cheat, either.

The lights went out on the block. I got up and took a leak and got back on my bunk. I got in the same place I was before and looked for the star. I found it right away. It was easier to find now because the lights was out. I got tired looking at it after a while and looked at another one. The other one was much more smaller and much more in a cluster. But I got tired of it after a while, too.

I thought about Munford. He said if they didn't get you in the cradle, they got you later. If they didn't suck all the manhood out of you in the cradle, they made you use it on people you didn't love. I never messed with a woman I didn't love. I always loved all these women I ever messed with. . . . No, I didn't love them. Because I didn't love her last night—I just wanted to fuck her. And I don't think I ever loved Marie, either. Marie just had the best pussy in the world. She had the best—still got the best. And that's why I went to her, the only reason I went. Because God knows she don't have any kind a face to make you come at her . . .

Maybe I ain't never loved nobody. Maybe I ain't never loved nobody since my mama died. Because I loved her, I know I loved her. But the rest—no, I never loved the rest. They don't let you love them. Some kind of way they keep you from loving them . . .

I have to stop thinking. That's how you go crazy—thinking. But what else can you do in a place like this—what? I wish I knowed somebody. I wish I knowed a good person. I would be good if I knowed a good person. I swear to God I would be good.

All of a sudden the lights came on, and I heard them bringing in somebody who was crying. They was coming toward the cell where I was; the person was crying all the way. Then the cell door opened and they throwed him in there and they locked the door again. I didn't look up—I wouldn't raise my head for nothing. I could tell nobody else was looking up, either. Then the footsteps faded away and the lights went out again.

I raised my head and looked at the person they had throwed in there. He was nothing but a little boy—fourteen or fifteen. He had on a white shirt and a pair of dark pants. Hattie helped him up off the floor and laid him on the bunk under me. Then he sat on the bunk 'side the boy. The boy was still crying.

"Shhh now, shhh now," Hattie was saying. It was just like a woman saying it. It made me sick a' the stomach. "Shhh now, shhh now," he kept on saying.

I swung to the floor and looked at the boy. Hattie was sitting on the bunk, passing his hand over the boy's face.

"What happened?" I asked him.

He was crying too much to answer me.

"They beat you?" I asked him.

He couldn't answer.

"A cigarette?" I said.

"No—no—sir," he said.

I lit one, anyhow, and stuck it in his mouth. He tried to smoke it and started coughing. I took it out.

"Shhh now," Hattie said, patting his face. "Just look at his clothes. The bunch of animals. Not one of them is a man. A bunch of pigs—dogs—philistines."

"You hurt?" I asked the boy.

"Sure, he's hurt," Hattie said. "Just look at his clothes, how they beat him. The bunch of dogs."

I went to the door to call the guard. But I stopped; I told myself to keep out of this. He ain't the first one they ever beat and he won't be the last one, and getting in it will just bring you a dose of the same medicine. I turned around and looked at the boy. Hattie was holding the boy in his arms and whispering to him. I hated what Hattie was doing much as I hated what the law had done.

"Leave him alone," I said to Hattie.

"The child needs somebody," he said. "You're going to look after him?"

"What happened?" I asked the boy.

"They beat me," he said.

"They didn't beat you for nothing, boy."

He was quiet now. Hattie was patting the side of his face and his hair.

"What they beat you for?" I asked him.

"I took something."

"What you took?"

"I took some cakes. I was hungry."

"You got no business stealing," I said.

"Some people got no business killing, but it don't keep them from killing," Hattie said.

150

He started rocking the boy in his arms the way a woman rocks a child.

"Why don't you leave him alone?" I said.

He wouldn't answer me. He kept on.

"You hear me, whore?"

"I might be a whore, but I'm not a merciless killer," he said.

I started to crack him side the head, but I changed my mind. I had already raised my fist to hit him, but I changed my mind. I started walking. I was smoking the cigarette and walking. I walked, I walked, I walked. Then I stood at the head of the bunk and look up at the window at the stars. Where was the one I was looking at a while back? I smoked on the cigarette and looked for it—but where was it? I threw the cigarette in the toilet and lit another one. I smoked and walked some more. The rest of the place was quiet. Nobody had said a word since the guards throwed that little boy in the cell. Like a bunch of roaches, like a bunch of mices, they had crawled in they holes and pulled the cover over they head.

All of a sudden I wanted to scream. I wanted to scream to the top of my voice. I wanted to get them bars in my hands and I wanted to shake, I wanted to shake that door down. I wanted to let all these people out. But would they follow me—would they? Y'all go'n follow me? I screamed inside. Y'all go'n follow me?

I ran to my bunk and bit down in the cover. I bit harder, harder, harder. I could taste the dry sweat, the dry piss, the dry vomit. I bit harder, harder, harder . . .

I got on the bunk. I looked out at the stars. A million little white, cool stars was out there. I felt my throat hurting. I felt the water running down my face. But I gripped my mouth tight so I wouldn't make a sound. I didn't make a sound, but I cried. I cried and cried and cried.

I knowed I was going to the pen now. I knowed I was going, I knowed I was going. Even if Medlow came to get me, I wasn't leaving with him. I was go'n do like Munford said. I was going there and I was go'n sweat it and I was go'n take it. I didn't want have to pull cover over my head every time a white man did something to a black boy—I wanted to stand. Because they never let you stand if they got you out. They didn't let Jack stand—and I had never heard of them letting anybody else stand, either.

I felt good. I laid there feeling good. I felt so good I wanted to sing. I sat up on the bunk and lit a cigarette. I had never smoked a cigarette like I smoked that one. I drawed deep, deep, till my chest got big. It felt good. It felt good deep down in me. I jumped to the floor feeling good.

"You want a cigarette?" I asked the boy.

I spoke to him like I had been talking to him just a few minutes ago, but it was over an hour. He was laying in Hattie's arms quiet like he was half asleep.

"No, sir," he said.

I had already shook the cigarette out of the pack.

"Here," I said.

"No, sir," he said.

"Get up from there and go to your own bunk," I said to Hattie.

"And who do you think you are to be giving orders?"

I grabbed two handsful of his shirt and jerked him up and slammed him 'cross the cell. He hit against that bunk and started crying—just laying there, holding his side and crying like a woman. After a while he picked himself up and got on that bunk.

"Philistine," he said. "Dog—brute."

When I saw he wasn't go'n act a fool and try to hit me, I turned my back on him.

"Here," I said to the boy.

"I don't smoke—please, sir."

"You big enough to steal?" I said. "You'll smoke it or you'll eat it." I lit it and pushed it in his mouth. "Smoke it."

He smoked and puffed it out. I sat down on the bunk 'side him. The freak was sitting on the bunk 'cross from us, holding his side and crying.

"Hold that smoke in," I said to the boy.

He held it in and started coughing. When he stopped coughing I told him to draw again. He drawed and held it, then he let it out. I knowed he wasn't doing it right, but this was his first time, and I let him slide.

"If Medlow come to get me, I'm not going," I said to the boy. "That means T. J. and his boys coming, too. They go'n beat me because they think I'm a smart aleck trying to show them up. Now you listen to me, and listen good. Every time they come for me I want you to start praying. I want you to pray till they bring me back in this cell. And I don't want you praying like a woman, I want you to pray like a man. You don't even have to get on your knees; you can lay on your bunk and pray. Pray quiet and to yourself. You hear me?"

He didn't know what I was talking about, but he said, "Yes, sir," anyhow.

"I don't believe in God," I said. "But I want you to believe. I want you to believe He can hear you. That's the only way I'll be able to take those beatings—with you praying. You understand what I'm saying?"

"Yes, sir."

"You sure, now?"

"Yes, sir."

I drawed on the cigarette and looked at him. Deep in me I felt some kind of love for this little boy.

"You got a daddy?" I asked him.

"Yes, sir."

"A mama?"

"Yes, sir."

"Then how come you stealing?"

" 'Cause I was hungry."

"Don't they look after you?"

"No, sir."

"You been in here before?"

"Yes, sir."

"You like it in here?"

"No, sir. I was hungry."

"Let's wash your back," I said.

We got up and went to the facebowl. I helped him off with his shirt. His back was cut from where they had beat him.

"You know Munford Bazille?" I asked him.

"Yes, sir. He don't live too far from us. He kin to you?"

"No, he's not kin to me. You like him?"

"No, sir, I don't like him. He stay in fights all the time, and they always got him in jail."

"That's how you go'n end up."

"No, sir, not me. 'Cause I ain't coming back here no more."

"I better not ever catch you in here again," I said. "Hold onto that bunk—this might hurt."

"What you go'n do?"

"Wash them bruises."

"Don't mash too hard."

"Shut up," I told him, "and hold on."

I wet my handkerchief and dabbed at the bruises. Every time I touched his back, he flinched. But I didn't let that stop me. I washed his back good and clean. When I got through, I told him to go back to his bunk and lay down. Then I rinched out his shirt and spread it out on the foot of my bunk. I took off my own shirt and rinched it out because it was filthy.

I lit a cigarette and looked up at the window. I had talked big, but what was I going to do when Medlow came? Was I going to change my mind and go with him? And if I didn't go with Medlow, I surely had to go with T. J. and his boys. Was I going to be able to take the beatings night after night? I had seen what T. J. could do to your back. I had seen it on this kid and I had seen it on other people. Was I going to be able to take it?

I don't know, I thought to myself. I'll just have to wait and see.

Bloodline

BLOODLINE

1: I figured it was about time she was coming to work, so I went to the door to look out for her. There she was, pushing the gate open and coming in the yard. She had on her long gray dress and the blue gingham apron. The apron was almost long as the dress and almost the same color —she had washed it so many times. She had on her big yellow straw hat, and I could see piece of the white rag on her head sticking out from under the hat. I stood in the shop door with a file and a plowshare and watched 'Malia come up the walk. She walked slow and tired, like any moment she might stop and go back. When she came in the shade of that big pecan tree, she raised her head and looked toward the tool shop. She knowed I'd be standing there.

"Making it on up, huh?" I said.

"Trying to," she said, and stopped to catch her breath.

Every morning when she came up to the yard like this, she stopped and we had a few words. Sometimes I went out in the yard where she was, sometimes I talked with her from the door. This morning I went out there because I wanted to ask her about that boy. I still had the file and the plowshare in my hand.

"I see Copper didn't come with you," I said.

"No," she said.

"No more than I expected from him," I thought to myself.

'Malia turned around and looked back toward the gate.

"That little incline getting steeper and steeper," she said.

"It get little steeper every day now, 'Malia," I said.

"Yes, Lord," she said.

It wasn't much of a incline. To them children who came to the yard to pick figs and pecans, it wasn't a incline at all. They could run it just like running on flat ground. But when you got old as she was—she was seventy-two, I was seventy—everything looked like a incline. Even walking downhill looked like a incline.

"Well, I better get on up there," she said, looking toward the house now. But she still didn't move, just standing there looking at the house behind the trees. You couldn't see much of the house for the moss hanging on the trees.

"How is he in there?" I asked her.

"Same," she said.

"He didn't come out yesterday."

"He wasn't feeling too strong," she said.

"You think this the last go round, 'Malia?"

"I hope not," she said. She spoke like she was very, very tired. "If it is, God pity every last one of us."

"She'll really let them Cajuns take over, won't she?"

"Won't she," 'Malia said.

"If Copper was white, then this plantation would go to him, not to her," I was thinking to myself. "But he's the wrong color to go round claiming plantations."

"Is Copper coming here at all today?" I asked 'Malia.

"No," she said.

"You told him Mr. Frank wanted to see him?"

"I told him," she said, looking up at me. I could see she was worried and scared. " 'Not that back door,' he said. 'Not that back door?' I said. 'I been going through that back door nigh on fifty years, Copper.' 'That's not for me,' he said. 'What would my soldiers say if they caught me going through a back door?' "

'Malia looked at me a long time after she had said this. I could see she was worried and scared.

"Soldiers, 'Malia?" I said. "His soldiers?"

"Something disturbing Copper, Felix," she said. "When he talk he don't look right. He looking at you, but he ain't seeing you. This morning we was talking at the table, but he wasn't hearing me. He was just sitting there, looking out that door, looking far 'way."

"This part about the soldiers," I said; "you sure he said soldiers?"

"He said soldiers," she said.

Then she started crying. I held the file and the plowshare in one hand, and I put my other arm round her shoulders.

"Here," I said. "Here, now."

"I don't know what's the matter," she said. "God knows, I did all I could."

"Why'd he come back here, 'Malia?" I asked, after she stopped crying.

She wiped her eyes with the palm of her hand and shook her head.

"He didn't tell you?"

"No," she said. "He just talk."

"About what, 'Malia?"

"The earth for everybody. Just like the sun for everybody. Just like the stars for everybody."

"You think he got anything in mind?"

"Don't talk like that, Felix."

"They doing that everywhere else, 'Malia. Everywhere else but here."

"That's not it," she said. "That can't be it. God knows, I

don't hope to see that day." She looked toward the house again. "I better get on up there," she said. "Feel like I just want drop. I just want lay down and rest."

"Why don't you go back home, 'Malia? I'll take word you don't feel good."

"No, I'll make it," she said. "It won't be too much longer."

I watched her go toward the house. She was walking slow, with her head down. After she went in the little yard, I couldn't see her again till she went up the back stairs. It took her so long to go up the stairs, I thought she had sat down to rest. Then I saw her pulling open the screen door and going in. I went back to the shop and filed on my plowshare. Nobody told me to do things like that, but since I lived on the man's place and didn't have to pay rent, and since I didn't have nothing else to do but lay round the house if I stayed home, I came up there every day and worked to keep myself busy. While I was in the shop, I thought about that boy in the quarters. I thought about his mon and his paw, Walter Laurent. That was one, that Walter. A black woman, no matter who she was, didn't have a chance if he wanted her. He didn't care if it was in the field, in the quarters, the store or that house; when he got his dick up, he hopped on any of them. But them days are gone now, just like he's gone. That black stallion saw to that.

2: After I finished my plowshare, I hung it against the wall with all the other things. I had a little bit of everything there—cane knives, axes, shovels, hoes, scy' blades, yo-yo blades, clod-chopper discs—anything you cared to name, I had it. Every time I found something kind of rusty and needed working over, I brought it to the shop and cleaned it up. Once, there, this was my special job. From Monday morning till Saturday night, my job was to keep everything in good shape to work in the field. Ah, but that was long, long ago. Now all the old ones are dying, and the young ones are leaving—and the Cajuns are taking over a little more every year. So I came up to the yard now just to keep the old hands busy. Because once the hands had stopped, the man wasn't no more.

I hadn't been in the shop more than half an hour when I heard that yellow gal, Dee-Dee, calling me out there in the yard. I went to the door to see what she wanted.

"He want you in there," she said, pointing toward the house.

"Who want me where?" I said.

"Mr. Frank," she said, pointing.

I went back in the shop to put up the hammer I had been working with, then I came back out there where she was. She was standing in a clump of bull grass waiting for me. That little white dress she wore wasn't just short, it was so thin you could see drawers and everything else under it.

"What's he want in there?" I asked her.

"I don't know," she said. "Just say come out here and find you."

"Ain't Stateman in there?"

"He in there begging with his clean-head self," she said.

"You ought to give Stateman what he want," I said. "Make yourself a nice little piece of change."

"Huh," she said. "Bet he die 'fore I let him crawl on top of me."

We went through the little gate and up the back stairs. Dee-Dee stopped in the kitchen and told me to go on to the dining room. Frank Laurent was sitting at the table eating breakfast when I came in there. He was dressed in his purple silk robe. He looked awful sick and weak that morning.

Frank was in his late sixties. He had suffered a heart attack about five years ago, and the doctor told him he had to hire a' overseer or give this place over to his niece to operate. He hired the overseer like the doctor said, but a few months later he fired him. He tried to manage the place by himself again and suffered another attack. The doctor told him the next one could kill him. So he hired another overseer, and this one was still there. The trouble was, though, the overseer had little to do with running the place outside of keeping a' eye on the Cajuns to make sure they didn't cheat Frank out of everything. He didn't have any say-so over the colored people in the quarters (since they wasn't share-cropping), and the only time he ever came up to the house was when Frank sent for him, and Frank sent for him least as he could.

Frank was the last of the old Laurents. When he died, the place was going to fall to his niece there in Bayonne. Besides the overseer and the doctor, his niece was the only other white person to come to the house. Every time she came there she told Frank he ought to go to the hospital where the doctors could give him the kind of treatment he needed. But Frank and all of us knowed that all she wanted was to get him out of that house so she could take over. After she did that, that was going to be the end of us. We was going to have to pay rent or we was going to have to leave. I doubt if half of the people on the place could do either one.

"You sent for me, Mr. Frank?" I said.

He didn't even look at me. He went on eating like I wasn't even there. 'Malia came in with a cup of coffee. She had taken off her straw hat, but she still had the white rag on her head. She put the cup of coffee in front of Frank, then she stood behind the chair looking at me and shaking her head. I could tell they had had some kind of squabble before I came in.

"Go get that boy," Frank said, pushing his plate back and pulling the cup in.

"Sir?" I said.

He didn't say any more. He raised the cup to his mouth. I didn't move.

"Are you deaf, Felix?" he said.

"Mr. Frank, I done already said Copper ain't coming through that back door," 'Malia said.

"You shut up back there," Frank said. "Well?" he said to me.

" 'Malia's right," I said.

"What?" Frank said.

"Copper's not coming through that back door, Mr. Frank," I said.

He looked straight in my eyes a long time, then he said: "You getting tired of this place, Felix? Tired beating on that one piece of iron day in and day out; year in and year out?"

"No sir," I said.

"You must be," Frank said. "I'd say you must be awful tired, Felix."

"Not a bit," I said. "I just want you to know the facts about Copper."

Frank tried to look hard, but he knowed I knowed all that hardness had gone. The plantation had taken all that hardness out of him when the others died and left it there for him to manage. It was too heavy for him. When something's too heavy, it makes most people wild animals or it breaks them. The land had broken Frank. It had aged him too fast. It had given him two heart attacks—and the next one was going to kill him. He knowed I knowed all of this. He knowed I knowed he wasn't hard, he was helpless. But he was still the authority there, and when he spoke I was supposed to move.

"You better get down the quarters," he said.

"Can I ask why, Mr. Frank?"

"Why?" he said. "Why? He's on my place, that's why. Any nigger on this place moves when I say move. He's no different from any of the rest."

"Ain't he, Mr. Frank?"

Frank didn't say anything. He raised the cup, and looked at me over the rim of the cup.

"I'll tell him you sent for him," I said. "Who I'm suppose to say?"

"You forgot my name, Felix?"

"No sir. I just thought you might want me to say his uncle, though."

"You pushing your luck, Felix, you know that, don't you?"

I nodded. "I reckon so."

I looked at 'Malia standing behind the chair, and I could see she wanted to cry again. I went out in the hall; there was Stateman with his head shining and his eyes rolling. He wanted to know what was happening in the dining room. When I told him to go in there and ask Frank himself, he looked at me real hard and turned away. He was Frank's butler, he had been there ever since Frank suffered his first heart attack; but me and 'Malia had been there almost long as Frank had been there, and he told us more than he ever told anybody else. And that's why he never scared me. I obeyed his orders because I respected him; not because I was scared of him.

3: 'Malia's house was the first one in the quarters, a little gray house that hadn't been painted in ages. She had two little chinaball trees and a mulberry tree in the front yard. In the morning, the trees had shade on the gallery. In the evening, the sun was behind the house, so 'Malia still had shade on the gallery. Hot as it was now, you needed shade or you couldn't sit outside at all.

Before I got to the house, I could see that boy standing on the gallery looking at me. When I got closer I saw he was dressed all in khakis. He even had on brown Army shoes—the shoes shining like new tin. I unhooked the gate and went in the yard—but I never got up the steps. I didn't even make a 'tempt to go up the steps. That boy's face stopped me: his eyes stopped me. His eyes looked hard as marble. I'm sure he knowed why I was there even before I opened my mouth.

"Mr. Frank want you to come visit him," I said from the ground.

He didn't say anything—just standing there in that Army uniform, looking down at me. He looked more like Walter Laurent than Walter ever looked like himself. Tall, slim, with a long face just like Walter. Only difference was, he was brown with curly black hair; his paw was white with straight brown hair.

"Go back and tell my uncle Generals don't go through back doors," he said.

"Tell him what?"

He didn't say any more, he just looked at me. He looked at me the same way any the other Laurents would 'a' looked at me. No, he looked at me the way Walter would 'a' looked at me if he had told me to do something and I had asked him what. You didn't ask a Laurent what; you did what the Laurent said.

"You're his adjutant, aren't you?" he said.

"His what?"

He gave me that Laurent look again. For a few seconds he might 'a' been thinking about something else: I was so little in his sight.

"His runner?" he said.

"He told me to come find you, and that's all I know."

"No one *comes* for the General," he said.

Then soon as he said it he wasn't looking at me any more, he was looking past me, his eyes hard as marble. I didn't know what to do after that. I didn't know if I ought to speak to him again or turn around and go back to the house. I lowered my head a second, and when I looked up, I saw him pulling a tablet and a pencil out of his Army shirt pocket. (The uniform was starched and pressed with all the creases. I'm sure this was the first time he had put it on since he got it out the cleaners.) He started writing with his left hand fast, just like Walter. He wrote about a minute. When he got through, he folded the piece of paper and held it out toward me. He didn't reach it out—I mean he didn't bend over and handed it to me; he just held it out. I went up the steps to get it, and my hand was shaking.

After I had gone out of the yard and had hooked the gate back, I looked up at him again. He wasn't looking at me now, he was looking down the quarters. But from the way his face was set, I doubt if he was seeing a thing.

4: When I got back to the house, I pulled the kitchen door open real quietly. There was Stateman, with his head shining, trying to feel up that yellow gal. He jumped back when he saw me and made 'tend he wasn't doing anything.

"You want me to give Mr. Frank a message or something?" he asked.

"No, that's all right," I said. "Just go on and try to get what you was trying to get before I came in. Mr. Frank and 'Malia still in the dining room?" I asked Dee-Dee.

"And what I was trying to get?" Stateman said.

"They in the library," Dee-Dee said.

"Don't get things mixed up round here, now," Stateman said. "If I was trying to get something you say I was trying to get, I wouldn't need a thing like you to tell me I was trying to get it."

I left him there and went up the hall to the library.

'Malia was sitting in one corner sewing a dress; Frank was in another corner reading a book. Both of them was sitting by a lamp. The big window between them was opened, but a tree outside the window always kept the room dark and cool. Frank looked up from his book and squinted his eyes when he didn't see Copper standing there with me.

"He sent you this," I said, carrying him the note.

Frank looked straight in my face all the time I was walking toward him. Even after he took the note, he still looked at me a long time before he lowered his eyes to read it. His face didn't change once all the time he was reading. He must 'a' read it two or three times before he looked up again.

"You wrote this, Felix?" he said.

He must 'a' been joking. I hadn't written a letter in my life, and he knowed that.

"Me?" I said.

"I see," he said. "You got him to do it."

But he didn't believe that, either. He said it because he couldn't think of anything else to say. He said it because Copper had sent him a note instead of coming here himself.

"All I did was tell him what you said," I said. "He did the rest."

"Sure," he said.

He knowed that's what had happened, but he didn't know Copper, and so he had to put it on me. He looked down at the note.

" 'My Dear Uncle,' " he said. He kept his eyes on the note another second, then he looked up at me. "He calls me 'Dear Uncle.' "

I shifted my feet a little, but I didn't say anything. Frank squinted up at me, with his mouth twisted a little to the side. He did this probably half a minute, then he looked down at the note again.

" 'My Dear Uncle,' " he said. He passed the tips of his finger and his thumb over the corners of his mouth, then he touched at his chest. " 'My Dear Uncle,' " he said again. " 'Let us speak General to General, gentleman to gentleman, Laurent to Laurent. I am sure you did not understand my position as a General, as a leader of men, when you invited me to your house through the back door. I believe you had in mind one of your slaves in the quarters, or one of your Cajun sharecroppers on the river; but not me. If I thought you meant that invitation, I would tell you, without hesitation, where to put that back door. But I am sure you did not mean it, therefore I have forgotten about it. If you wish to send me any other messages—an apology, or an invitation to speak to me as a General, as a Laurent, you can send the message to me in the quarters. I shall be there reconnoitering the area. Your respectful kin, General Christian Laurent.' "

Frank kept his head down another minute, like he was reading the note all over again. Then he squinted up at me and twisted his mouth slightly to the left.

"Is this boy crazy, or do you all think it was time you took over?"

"Took over?" I said. "I don't know what you talking about, Mr. Frank."

"Who sent for Copper?"

"Sent for him? Nobody sent for Copper," I said. "Nobody knowed where that boy was since his mon died there."

He knowed I was telling him the truth, but he wanted me to believe he thought different.

"This General—what does he mean by General? And Laurent—doesn't he know better than to say things like that round here?"

"I just brought the note," I said.

"And you're innocent as a baby, huh, Felix? You want me to believe that?"

"Believe what you want, Mr. Frank," I said. "I didn't

have nothing to do with Copper coming back here."

"You getting smart with me, Felix?"

"No sir," I said, and I lowered my eyes.

"And you?" I heard him asking 'Malia. Now he had to bring her in it, too. "How innocent are you?"

"Mr. Frank, till Copper showed up here yesterday, I hadn't seen him or heard from him in ten years. Since his mon died."

"So everybody is innocent, is that it?" he said. "That nigger comes here calling himself a Laurent, calling himself a General, walking over my place like he owns it—and everybody is innocent? I'm supposed to believe that?"

It was quiet in the room while Frank looked at me and 'Malia.

"Felix, go over to that store and get me two of the biggest niggers you can find," he said. "Saturday, there ought to be a dozen of them over there."

5: There wasn't a dozen round the store, but there was seven or eight of them there. Frank, Alcie and Tom-Tom was playing cards on the end of the gallery. Pool-Doo, Crowley and Simon was drinking soda water under that big pecan tree in front of Mr. Pichot house. Joby and Little Boy was sitting on the steps talking. Mr. Pichot, the old Cajun who ran the store, sat by the door in his chair. He had the chair cocked back against the wall, and his feet wasn't touching the floor.

"Little Boy, you and Joby, Mr. Frank want y'all," I said, after I had spoke to everybody.

"Who—us—for what?" Little Boy said. "What we done?"

"Come on," I said.

"Lord, have mercy," Little Boy said. "Now, what? People can't even rest round here on Saturday."

They followed me round the store back to the house.

Little Boy was grumbling all the way; Joby was keeping quiet. When we came in the kitchen, I saw Stateman ducking down the hall. I supposed he had been trying to feel up that yellow gal again.

"What's this?" she said, when she saw Little Boy and Joby.

"How I'm supposed to know," Little Boy said. "They don't tell nobody nothing."

Dee-Dee started laughing, and we left her back there laughing. I knocked on the library door, and when 'Malia told us to come in, I nodded for Little Boy and Joby to go in first. Little Boy and Joby, both of them with their hats in their hands, stood before Frank Laurent like two little children. 'Malia, in her corner, went on sewing like nothing was happening. Poor 'Malia was so tired, and she had seen so much foolishness, things like this didn't bother her much any more.

"You two niggers stay on my place?" Frank asked.

"Course we do, Mr. Frank," Little Boy said. "You know us."

"Do I?" Frank said. "The only thing I know is that somebody's running round this place telling me where I can put that back door, and I—"

"No sir, no sir," Little Boy said. "I didn't say that—I didn't. But Joby, he could 'a'. 'Cause just like you see him standing there, Joby got a big mouth. I done told Joby, I done told Joby—I said, 'Joby, mind your mouth; mind your mouth, boy, or one of these good days it go'n get you in a lot of trouble.' I told him that no later than, I think, last Sunday." He turned to Joby. "Didn't I tell you that?"

"I don't 'member you telling me nothing," Joby said.

"I did tell you that, Joby."

"You didn't," Joby said. " 'Cause I didn't see you Sunday. I seen you Saturday."

"Then I told you Saturday," Little Boy said. "I knowed it was one of them days."

"Where you told me that at?" Joby said. "Where? At the fair? At the road? In Bayonne? Where? The store?"

"In one of them places," Little Boy said. "I can't 'member everything."

"You ain't told me nothing," Joby said. He turned toward Frank, and I could see he wanted to cry. "Mr. Frank, I swear by my mama Little Boy ain't told me nothing."

Frank had been squinting up at them all the time they stood there squabbling. Even after they quit, he still looked at them a long time before he said anything.

"You two mind if I go on now?" he said.

Little Boy looked at Frank, but Joby lowered his head. He was waiting to hear the punishment Frank was going to give him.

"Either of you know Copper?" Frank asked.

"Miss Amalia's nephew?" Little Boy said, pointing toward 'Malia in the corner. "Yes sir, I know him. He's down the quarters right now."

"Go down there and bring him back up here," Frank said. "I don't want any scars on him, I don't want any broken bones, but I want him up here."

"Yes sir," Little Boy said. Then he turned to 'Malia. "Hope that's all right with you, Miss Amalia?"

"What did you ask her?" Frank said.

"I was just telling Miss Amalia over there I hope it's all right with her if—" Little Boy stopped.

"You're asking *her* if it's all right when *I* told you to do something?" Frank asked him.

"I wouldn't want do nothing she might not—" Little Boy stopped again before he finished.

"Do like Mr. Frank say," 'Malia said, with her head down.

"Just a minute," Frank said. "Who the hell's running this place, me or Amalia?"

"I guess you, Mr. Frank," Little Boy said.

"You guess, nigger?" Frank said. "You guess?"

Little Boy lowered his head, but Frank kept on looking at him. Then all of a sudden his face changed. Like only now he re'lized, maybe he wasn't running the place. Maybe somebody else *was* running it after all. Or, maybe nobody was running it. Maybe it was just running down.

"Get out of here," he said.

"Yes sir," Little Boy said. "Joby, come on."

They went out. I started to follow them, but Frank stopped me. I turned toward him with my cap in my hand.

"This whole place gone mad?" he said.

I didn't answer him.

"You hear me talking to you, Felix, goddamn it," he said.

"It ain't mad, Mr. Frank," I said. "It ain't no more like it used to be, that's all."

"What you're trying to say is that I'm not running this place any more? You and Amalia are?"

"Nobody's running the place, Mr. Frank," I said. "The Cajuns sharecropping it, and the overseer seeing that—"

"I'm running it, damn you," he said. "I'm running it."

I nodded. "Yes sir."

Then that look came on his face again. "I'm not running nothing," it said. "They know I'm not running nothing; I know I'm not running nothing."

"Why did they have to leave me here?" he said out loud. "Why did I have to be the one to stay?"

"Now, stop that," 'Malia said.

"Why?" he said again. "Why? I wanted no part of it. Why did they have to dump it on my lap?"

"You have relatives there," 'Malia said. "She'd be glad to take it off your hands."

"Is that what you all want, for her to take it over?" he asked 'Malia. He looked at 'Malia a while, but she went on sewing. "Is that what you want?" he said. "And do you know what'll happen then? She would kick you off the place before I was cold in my grave. She would let the Cajuns plow up the ground where your houses are now. And that cemetery back there, what do you think'll happen to it? Do you think she would hesitate a moment before she plowed that under too? Do you have another plot of land picked out for the bones, Amalia? Now, do you know why I go on?"

"Vexing yourself like that won't let you go on much longer," 'Malia said.

"I was all right until that nigger got here," Frank said. "Until your nephew got here, Amalia."

"Us nephew," 'Malia said softly, with her head down.

"What did you say?" Frank asked her. "What did you say, Amalia?"

She kept her head down; she didn't answer him.

"I heard you," Frank said. "You joining Felix and that nigger, too, huh?"

'Malia raised her head and looked at him. "Ain't that's why you want Copper here, Mr. Frank?" she said.

"That nigger is on my place," Frank said. "Any nigger on my place comes to my house when I say come."

"Look like Mr. Walter got plenty more round here nobody ain't been sending for," 'Malia said.

Frank got whiter. 'Malia had never talked to him like that before. If she wasn't so tired, and if Copper hadn't had her so mixed up, I'm sure she wouldn't 'a' talked like that now. Frank raised his hand real slowly, then he pushed it inside the robe quickly and rubbed his chest. He was breathing fast and hard, like he was trying to catch his breath. 'Malia jumped up from the chair and ran to him.

"You all right?" she asked him. "You all right? You want your pills? You want the doctor? Mr. Frank? Mr. Frank, you hear me?"

He didn't answer her. His head was bowed. He rubbed his chest hard as he could.

"Mr. Frank?" 'Malia said. She turned to me. "Felix?"

"Sit down," Frank said, out of breath. He never raised his head. "Sit down."

'Malia moved back to her chair, but she didn't sit down. I just stood there watching. I didn't know what to do. After a while, Frank raised his head and looked at 'Malia.

"Did I frighten you?" he asked her. "What's the matter, Amalia? Did you hear the tractors knocking over the house?"

'Malia sat back down, but she kept on watching him. Frank rubbed his chest inside the robe. The room was absolutely quiet all this time.

"What does that nigger look like?" Frank asked me.

"Who, Copper?" I said. Because I was still thinking about what had just happened. And I could hear the tractors knocking over the houses and plowing up the graves.

"Who do you think I'm talking about, Felix?"

"He's a tall, slim boy," I said.

" 'He's a tall, slim boy,' " Frank said, mocking me. " 'He's a tall, slim boy.' Does he have hands? Is he green? Does he speak Russian?"

"He's brown," I said. "Gray eyes. A long face. He writes with his left hand."

"And because he writes with his left hand, he can't come through that back door?"

I didn't answer him.

"Well?" he said.

"That's why he won't come through that back door, Mr. Frank," I said.

"He'll come through that back door, and he'll be glad to come through that back door," Frank said. "You can go back to your hammering now."

"Thank you," I said, and turned to leave.

"That one piece of iron ought to be thin as a razor blade by now," Frank said.

I faced him again. "It's not the same piece," I said. "I got all that old stuff there."

"You've never told me why you stay in there so much," he said, squinting up at me.

"Maybe some day somebody'll use it again," I said.

"And who may that somebody be?" he said. "Copper?"

"I don't know, Mr. Frank," I said. "Maybe it will be Copper."

"Yes, maybe it will be Copper, Felix," Frank said. "But I'll be in my grave before that day comes."

6: I went to the store to get me a pack of tobacco, then I went back to the shop. I had done no more than picked up my file when I heard that yellow gal calling me out there again. When I got to the door, I saw her standing out there with a basket of clothes in her arms. She was on her way from the clothesline.

"Now, what?" I said.

"Samson been calling you," she said.

"Samson?" I said. "What—"

"Yonder," she said, pointing with the basket. "Look like he got Joby and Little Boy tied together."

Joby and Little Boy faced the gate like a pair of mules or a pair of oxen that had been working the fields all day. Samson was holding something behind them, but I didn't know what it was till I got closer. Then I saw it was the end of a trace chain, with the other end wrapped around both Joby and Little Boy. The first thing to come to my mind was a bad dog or a bull. "Yes, a bull," I thought; "a bull. Ben's bull. He got out the pasture and took after them. When they saw him coming, they tried to get under Samson's wire fence, but the fence was too low. But, wait," I thought. "Wait, now. I can see a bull running you under a wire fence and making you rip half your clothes off, but where would that bull get a chain from?"

Then Samson told me: Copper.

"Sure, sure," I thought. "Copper." Only it hadn't darted my mind that one human being would do that to two more of his own kind.

Samson told me what happened, then he gived me the end of the trace chain he was holding. Copper had tied their hands behind their back with their own belts.

"Maybe this'll convince him he don't want come up here," I said to Samson.

"I don't know 'bout him, but I'm sure you couldn't pay these here to go mess with him again," Samson said. "I done seen some fighting in my days, but I ain't never seen none like that young man can put up. Biff, boff; ooof, offf. You got to be possessed to fight like that."

"Let's go," I said to Joby and Little Boy. "Thanks, Samson."

"My pleasure," Samson said. "He paid me a quarter to bring them up here. Yes, you got to be possessed to fight like that. Boff, biff. Doggonest thing I ever seen in my life."

We started toward the house. That yellow gal was still out in the yard with that basket of clothes. When we came closer to her, she started laughing. She laughed so hard, she dumped half of the clothes out of the basket on the grass.

Stateman met us at the door; he said he didn't know if he could allow us to come in there, seeing the way we was looking. I pushed him to the side and nodded for Joby and Little Boy to go on up the hall. I knocked on the door, and when 'Malia told us to come in, I let them go in first.

'Malia made a loud groan and throwed her hand up to her mouth when she saw Little Boy and Joby. But Frank's expression didn't change. You would 'a' thought Stateman had just brought him a cold glass of water and that was all. After he had looked at Joby and Little Boy, he looked at the trace chain that tied them together. He looked at it the way you look at something, but you not really seeing it. The way you look at something, but at the same time you thinking about something else. Then he looked at 'Malia. 'Malia a while, then Joby and Little Boy again, then me. I'm sure he thought we was doing all this to either run him crazy or kill him. Then he probably thought maybe he ought to let us kill him. If we killed him, then he wouldn't have to go through the torment of keeping up this place day in and day out. He would be free of this place, free of us (who, he said, he never wanted), and he would be free of all his pains.

He covered his mouth to cough. Then he said pardon.

"Sir?" Little Boy asked, raising his head.

" 'Pardon,' " Frank said.

"Yes sir," Little Boy said, lowering his head again and jingling the chains.

Now, it got quiet again. All this time, Frank was waiting for me to start talking. He had been waiting for me to explain since we came in there. But I was waiting for him to ask me what had happened. He knowed what had happened, but he thought it was my place to start off first. Well, I wasn't going to say a word till he opened his mouth.

Then he couldn't hold back any more. He looked at me like I was the cause for all of this. He knowed I wasn't. He knowed it was Copper and just Copper. But since he couldn't reach Copper, he had to accuse me. Like a man who beat his mule because his wife beat him; or the man who go home and beat his child because the overseer cussed him out in the field.

"Well, Felix?" he said.

"All right, Little Boy," I said.

Little Boy started off, but Frank wasn't looking at Little Boy, he was still looking at me—still accusing me. Sure, he knowed I didn't have nothing to do with it, but since he couldn't touch Copper, he had to touch somebody else. It would 'a' been 'Malia if I wasn't there, but since I was, and since it was me who had brought the note from Copper, and since it was me who had brought Little Boy and Joby in there, then I had to be the one to blame.

". . . down there with that little brown tablet and that pencil, looking at Mr. Rufus old house," Little Boy was saying.

I looked at Little Boy again. His blue denim shirt looked like a line of ribbons. I'm sure if Samson hadn't told me what had happened, I would 'a' thought somebody had put Little Boy in a pit with a bobcat. Only, the person had tied Little Boy's hands behind his back and had told that bobcat to go to work on him.

". . . I went there and told him you wanted to see him," Little Boy was saying, "but he didn't pay me no mind. After he got through writing up the house, he jumped the ditch and sighted 'long the fence, then he jumped back and writ some more on that little tablet. He looked down at the ditch a little while and even writ something 'bout it, too."

"After he had pulled up piece of that jimpson weed and chewed it," Joby told Little Boy.

Joby lowered his head again. Little Boy nodded. The chain jingled when either one of them moved.

"Yeah," Little Boy said. "After he had pulled up piece of that jimpson weed and tasted it, he writ something 'bout it in that little tablet. Bitter or sweet, I don't know. Then after he got through there, he went down to Compaa house . . ."

Frank was looking at Little Boy, but you could see he was thinking about something else. Maybe he was thinking he was dreaming. Maybe he was thinking he was in a crazy house, or maybe he was dead and this was hell.

"I told him again you wanted to see him, but he just went right on writing," Little Boy said. "Acting more like he was white—like he was Mr. Walter—"

He stopped again. That was something he wasn't ever supposed to say. Anybody in the world who had ever seen Walter Laurent and saw Copper could see that Walter Laurent was Copper's paw. But you wasn't supposed to ever say it.

When Frank heard his brother's name, his eyes shifted a little. He had been looking at Little Boy all this time, but he hadn't been listening to him. But hearing Walter's name woke him up. He started looking at Joby and Little Boy like it was just that moment he re'lized they was in the room.

"Where did you meet the bears?" he said.

"B'ars, sir?" Little Boy said.

Frank nodded. "B'ars."

"Me and Joby ain't met no b'ars nowhere, sir," Little Boy said.

"Sure, you did," Frank said.

Little Boy and Joby looked at each other like two small children. They didn't know if to agree with Frank or not. To say yes, they met bears would 'a' been a lie, and they could be punished. To say no, they didn't meet any bears would 'a' been calling Frank a lie, and they could be punished for that, too. So they looked at each other, not saying a thing. For my part, all I wanted to do was laugh.

"I sent you and Joby down the quarters to find Copper," Frank said. "But Copper told both of you to go to hell. You didn't go to hell—no, you came back up here to tell me what Copper had said, and that's when you met the two bears. One grabbed you and threw you down, the other one grabbed Joby and did him the same. They took off your belts, wore out your butts, and tied your hands behind your backs. But that wasn't all. One of the bears happened to have a chain 'cross his shoulder. Where he got the chain from, we won't question. But he tied you and Joby together and sent you on your way."

Little Boy started shaking his head and giggling.

"Mr. Frank, you too much," he said.

Frank looked at 'Malia sitting in the other chair. He was probably wondering if he ought to accuse her of helping me and Copper. 'Malia just sat there with her head bowed. Poor woman.

"Me and Joby followed him down to Aunt Johnson after he got through writing up Compaa house, and I told him what you said again," Little Boy said. "He didn't pay me no mind, he just went right on writing. Aunt Johnson sitting out there on that gallery, looking at him, not saying a word. Just sitting there shelling beans in that lard bucket and smoking that corb pipe."

Frank looked from 'Malia to Little Boy. He was hearing Little Boy, but he was thinking about something else. Probably who Aunt Johnson was and what a corb pipe was. Then I could see, by the way his eyes shifted, he remembered Aunt Johnson was so and so—probably the old lady who used to come out to the store and argue with Mr. Pichot all the time. A corb pipe was probably a corn cob pipe.

"When he got through with her house, he went on down to Samson," Little Boy said. "It was there, in front of Samson, Joby, there, thought 'bout th'owing him down and toting him back up here."

Joby jerked up his head. "Me?" he said. "Me? How come it's always me? You the one say let's th'ow him down and car' him back up there. You the one. You. Not me. You."

"All right, I said it," Little Boy said. He turned to 'Malia. "I'm sorry, Miss Amalia."

'Malia looked in his face and looked at his clothes. His blue denim shirt was a line of ribbons, little ribbons and big ones. A big chunk of cloth was ripped from his left pant leg, and you could see a big cut just under his knee. After 'Malia had looked at him a moment, she nodded her head to show him she understood, and she lowered her eyes again.

"I tripped him over," Little Boy went on. "He jumped back up quicker than any human being you ever seen and slammed into Joby. Two quick chops 'cross Joby shoulder blade with the side of his hand, and down went Joby. I tried to grab him again, but the first thing I knowed I was tangled in Samson wire fence. Joby got up to help me, and the next thing I knowed Joby was tangled there, too.

"He made us untangle each other, then he made us take off us belts and he tied us hands behind us back. He told Samson to bring him a chain or a rope. Samson leaned the broom 'gainst the wall and went out in the back yard and brought a chain like he said. He tied us together with the chain and gived Samson a quarter to bring us up here. The last thing I seen, he was sharpening that pencil again."

"How much did Copper pay you niggers to come back up here with that tale?" Frank asked.

"Pay us?" Joby said, jerking up his head and jingling the chains. "Pay us? He didn't pay nobody but Samson."

"How much is Felix paying you?" Frank asked.

Both of them looked at me like two scared children. Two men, both of them close to two hundred pounds, looking at me like two scared children. They didn't know what to say, what to think; they turned to Frank again.

"Do you know what Mr. Walter would have done with you two trifling niggers?"

Neither one of them answered him.

"Well?" he said.

"No sir," Little Boy said.

"He would have hanged one of you. Right out there in the yard. The other one would have gone back down there and brought Copper up here gently as a baby." He looked at them a long time to let his words soak in. "Get out of here," he said.

They turned to leave. I gived Little Boy the end of the chain I had been holding. They went out with the chain jingling.

Frank looked at me again.

"Go back to that store and get me six more," he said. "Hot as it is—Saturday, too—you probably have the whole plantation over there drinking soda water."

"Why don't you leave Copper 'lone, Mr. Frank," 'Malia said. "If he don't want come see you, I wouldn't force him. Leave him 'lone."

"Leave him alone, hell," Frank said. "Not on my place will I leave him alone. Get moving, you traitor."

"Mr. Frank, please," 'Malia said.

"Well?" he said to me.

"You the authority," I said, and went out.

"Is that any way to talk to Felix?" I heard 'Malia saying through the door. "Is that any way to talk to Felix? Who you got beside me and Felix, Mr. Frank? Who?"

"Nobody," I heard him saying.

7: More of them had gathered round the store when I came over there. If they wasn't laying on the gallery, they was standing under that big pecan tree to the side. All of them was talking about what had happened down the quarters. J. W. Hudson, that big-mouth boy of Aunt Jude Hudson, was leading the talk. He was showing everybody else what Little Boy and Joby had done wrong. They had gone on Copper wrong, he said. They shouldn't 'a' talked so much. They should 'a' just got him by surprise and brought him on back up the quarters.

I sat on the end of the gallery, smoking a cigarette and listening to J. W. By the time I had finished my cigarette, I figured Mr. J. W. had convinced everybody out there he knowed the best way to capture Copper. I went over to the tree and told him Frank wanted him at the house.

"Me? For what?" he said. "What I done?"

I didn't answer him. I counted out five more and told them to follow me.

When we came back to the house, that yellow gal was standing by the kitchen table wrapping a bandage over Little Boy's shoulder. She had bathed the scratches in Epsom-salt water, she had put salve on them, and now she was wrapping the shoulder with a piece of bar cloth. She had already fixed up Joby and he was standing to the side holding the trace chain.

"I guess he trying to get y'all killed now, huh?" Little Boy said.

"Be still," Dee-Dee said. "Letting one man beat two. Bet he couldn't beat you eating."

I knocked on the library door, and when 'Malia answered, I nodded for J. W. and his gang to go in. When the last one had stepped inside, I moved in and shut the door.

"You know why you're here?" Frank asked them.

"Copper, sir?" J. W. said.

"Yes. Copper. You know he's tough, don't you?"

"No one man can beat no six, Mr. Frank; I don't care how tough he is," J. W. said.

"I hope you're trying to convince me and not yourself," Frank said. "I want him brought up here. I don't care if you have to drag him from one end of the quarters to the other. If he get hooked in the fence, drag him through it. If you catch him hiding in somebody's house, drag him down the steps. But bring him back up here. Then stand him on his feet at the foot of those stairs. He will *walk* through that back door."

"He will, Mr. Frank," J. W. said. "You don't have to worry 'bout that."

"I'm not worrying," Frank said. "You worry if you don't get him up here."

"He'll be up here, sir. You can rest your mind on that."

Frank looked at J. W. a long time, like he wanted to be sure to remember him. J. W. couldn't take Frank's glaring at him, and he lowered his head.

"What's your name?" Frank asked.

J. W. raised his head. "I'm J. W., Mr. Frank," he said, grinning. "Renton Hudson boy."

"How is Renton?"

"Papa dead, Mr. Frank. Been dead couple years now. Mama, she living, though."

Frank nodded and grunted.

"You can leave," he said.

"Yes sir," J. W. said, and turned to the others. "Come on, fellows; let's go find that tush-hog."

They went out. I started to follow them, but Frank stopped me.

"Go back there and tell that gal to fix you up some food," he said. "Should be round your dinner time, shouldn't it?"

"Don't b'lieve I'm hungry," I said.

He wanted to make up for the way he had talked to me just before I went to get J. W., and I wanted him to know it wasn't going to be that easy.

"Well, you might as well sit down over there," he said.

"I was thinking I ought to get back in the shop," I said. "Since I ain't done too much today, yet."

"Can't you stay a minute?" he said. "Or do I have to beg you, too?"

"Sit down, Felix," 'Malia said quietly.

I went to the chair in the other corner, and I brushed off my pants before I sat down. It was the first time I had ever sat in the library, but I had sat in the living room two or three times when they had wakes there.

It was quiet in the room now. 'Malia went on stitching the dress. Frank went to the window to look out in the yard. Once there, I caught him rubbing at his chest. He was always doing that now. Like he had to do that to keep his heart beating.

"I didn't write the rules," he said, looking out the window. He wasn't talking to us, he was just talking out loud. "And I won't try to change them. He must come through that back door."

I looked at 'Malia in her corner, but she kept her head down. Frank turned from the window and looked at me.

"And you don't think he will?"

"No sir," I said. "Not him."

"You're pretty sure of that, aren't you, Felix? Aren't you?"

"Yes sir," I said. "Because you never would 'a' gone through a back door, Mr. Frank; neither Mr. Walter, neither y'all daddy."

"Keep talking, Felix."

"That's about all," I said.

"You didn't finish," Frank said. "You forgot to mention his mon, Felix. She was black."

"She born him, Mr. Frank, that's all," I said. "Copper is a Laurent. No Laurent's walking through any back door—'specially one he half figures belong to him, anyway."

"So you did send for him?" Frank said.

"No sir," I said. "No more than you or 'Malia did, Mr. Frank. But I took a good look at him when I went down to that house. And I looked at him yesterday when he got here. Not that one, Mr. Frank."

"We'll see," Frank said.

"Can I leave now?"

"You'll leave when I tell you to leave."

"You the authority," I said.

Then it got quiet again—too quiet. I looked at 'Malia stitching on the dress, but I could tell Frank was still looking at me from the window. I could tell he was mad, I could tell he was getting madder.

"What am I supposed to do?" he said, when he couldn't hold back any more. "Change the rules? Do you know how old these rules are? They're older than me, than you, than this entire place. I didn't make them, I came and found them here. And I—an invalid—am I supposed to change them all? Haven't I fed you when you were hungry, given you a place to sleep? If you're sick I give you medicine whether you have money or not. I don't charge you a penny rent, I don't charge a cent for the food you raise in your gardens. What more am I supposed to do—give you the house and move into the quarters? Do you think you'll live better then? Well?"

"You better watch your heart," 'Malia said, very softly, and never raising her head.

"To hell with my heart," Frank said. "To hell with you, the place, Felix—everything."

"That ain't being too smart," 'Malia said, still very softly, and still not looking at him.

"So today is my day to be criticized, eh?" he said. "Is that what it's coming to?"

"Nobody's trying to criticize you, Mr. Frank," 'Malia said. "I just said your heart."

"Like hell, nobody's trying to criticize me," Frank said. "What the hell's Felix been doing ever since he got up this morning?"

"Can I leave now?" I said.

"You start toward that door, Felix, so help me God I'll get that gun out of that desk drawer and shoot your goddamn head off."

"You the authority," I said.

"You must have the last damn word every time, mustn't you?" Frank said.

I got quiet. I could see he was mad.

"Ain't it 'bout time you had your dinner?" 'Malia said, to break the silence.

"I eat when I damned well please," Frank said, turning on 'Malia now. "I hope I still have that privilege in my own house." When 'Malia didn't say anything, he said: "Well, aren't you going to say, 'You the authority,' just to have the last word?"

"You know who you is, Mr. Frank," 'Malia said.

"I'm an invalid," he said. "I'm an invalid who everyone laughs at soon as my back is turned."

"I never laughed at you in my life, Mr. Frank," 'Malia said. "And I'm sure Felix never done either."

It got quiet again. I rubbed my hand over my old black cap I had hanging on my knee. Then I just looked at my hands a while. I guess I never would 'a' done that if I was out in the shop or at my own house. But in here, with all these books and furnitures and fine things, I just, all of a sudden, looked at both of my hands. How rough they looked. Knotted, old, hard, and wrinkled.

"How come you didn't protest?" Frank asked 'Malia.

"Protest what, Mr. Frank?"

"Their dragging him back up here, that's what."

"They ain't go'n drag Copper nowhere," she said.

"And why not?"

"I'm sure I don't need to even answer that, Mr. Frank," 'Malia said, with her head down.

"You better answer that, damn you," he said. "And I wish you would look up when I'm talking to you, Amalia."

'Malia stuck the needle in the dress and raised her head.

"Copper both of us nephew, Mr. Frank," she said. "And they know that. And they know ain't nowhere in the world for them to go if they hurt him."

"You and Felix seem to be throwing that nephew stuff pretty heavily round here today," Frank said. "You better mind your tongue doesn't slip at the wrong time."

"I know my place," 'Malia said.

"Do you?" Frank said. "I thought you had forgotten it. For a moment there, I thought everybody in here was white."

"No sir, I'm not white," she said.

"You sure now?"

"I'm sure, Mr. Frank. You the only white person in here."

"Thank you," he said, nodding his head.

Somebody knocked on the door, and 'Malia told him to come in. Stateman pushed the door open and told Frank his dinner was ready. Frank left the window. A tall, slim man with thin, gray hair. A very weak man; a very sick man.

"Tell that gal to fix up something for Felix in the kitchen," he said to Stateman.

"Yes sir," Stateman said, standing to the side to let Frank go out first.

Frank stopped at the door and looked back at me.

"When you get through eating, you go to that living room and sit down," he said. "Don't you dare leave this house until I see that boy."

"You the authority," I said.

"And you keep remembering that, too," he said, and went out.

Stateman followed him.

"One ain't no better than the other one," 'Malia said. "They the same, that same blood in 'em. Didn't I used to sing at Copper and sing at Copper 'fore he left here. Him fighting them white children on the river like he fight them black ones in the quarter. Didn't I used to sing and sing and sing at him. My singing didn't do no good then; now he's back here doing worse."

"What I can't understand, what Mr. Frank want see him so bad for. If nobody wanted to see me, I sure wouldn't go through that much trouble to get him in my house."

"He know he's going to die soon," 'Malia said. "He want leave something for Copper in his will. In my name."

"Not this place, I'm sure?"

"Lord, no," 'Malia said. "Something small. Maybe no more than a few dollars."

"To pay for what Walter did to his mon?"

"I reckon so."

"But Copper got to come through the back to get it?"

"Yes," 'Malia said.

"He won't see that day," I said.

"Copper scares me, Felix," 'Malia said.

"How do you mean?"

"Look what he did Little Boy and Joby. Look how he beat them and put them in chains. He would do that to anybody who got in his way. I think he would even do that to me."

"Not to you—no," I said.

"Yes," she said. "To me. Something's in Copper. Something happened to Copper. Things he talk about. Rights. Wrongs. Soldiers. Generals. Who the earth for. Who the sun belongs to. That kind of talk scares me, Felix."

"Maybe he'll hurry up and go back," I said.

"I hope so," she said. Then she lowered her head and started crying. "My own blood—I want my own blood to leave my house."

I went to her and put my hand on her shoulder. I started to tell her it wasn't her blood making Copper act like that, but I didn't know if that was the thing to say then.

"Let's go eat something," I told her. "You ought to be hungry, too."

She stood up, and we went back in the kitchen.

8: When I finished eating, I went to the living room and sat down. It was a big room with big, old, dark furnitures. They had all the curtains drawn back, but still there wasn't enough light in there. The trees in the yard kept sun from ever getting into that house. I sat in a big, old, highback chair, facing the fireplace. No matter where you looked in the room, you saw pictures of the family. Pictures of soldiers everywhere—probably from all the wars. There was a picture of Greta Jean standing in front of the house with two young men on both sides of her. She looked happy as she could be, because she knowed she was going to get this place after Frank died. On the mantelpiece was a picture of Walter on that stallion, Black Terror. And how I remember them two. I remembered how he used to race that horse through the quarters and how the people had to fall out his way when they heard him coming. I remembered how he used to pick fights with the colored boys in the field for no reason at all—just for the sake of fighting them. And the women, married or single—what did he care? They was on his place and they belong to him. And nobody, white or black, would dare tell him he was wrong. It took that horse he loved to stop him. One day, just before a storm, he rode the horse back in the field. Something scared the horse—probably a clap of thunder—and the horse threw him from the saddle. But he never got his foot out of the stirrup, and the horse dragged him all the way to the front. I still remembered how I heard that horse's hoofs pounding that hard ground, coming back to the yard. Will Henderson saw him first and started hollering: "Head him. Head him. He dragging Mr. Walter. Head him." We stopped the horse, all right, but by the time we got Walter loose from the stirrup, he was already dead. His back and his skull, both broke.

For a long time, I couldn't take my eyes off that picture.

But I wasn't thinking about Walter and that horse; I was thinking about that other one running round in the quarters, calling himself a General and a Laurent. "They the same two," I told myself. "It's Walter back."

I had been in the room a good half an hour when Frank came in. Then I saw what had kept him so long: he had changed clothes. He had put on a pair of gray pants, a white shirt, and a little polka-dotted bow tie. To get dressed up like that had taken all the little strength he had. He looked so weak and white now, I thought he was going to fall before he got to that chair. 'Malia came in a few minutes later with her sewing and sat by a lamp in the corner. She still had the white rag on her head. Long time ago, all the house servants had to wear a rag on their heads all the time. But now the people in the big houses didn't make them do it unless they wanted to. 'Malia still did it, just like she had done it thirty, forty years back.

Nobody said anything to anybody. 'Malia was sewing and humming a song to herself. I couldn't hear all of the song, just a word now and then. I had hung my old leather cap on my knee, and I passed my hand over the cap every time I caught Frank looking over there at me. Frank took out his watch and glanced at the time.

"Maybe they had to tree him," he said.

Then it got quiet again. I didn't feel right at all in there. I wanted to get back to my shop and sharpen up something. A man used to the outside don't feel right cooped up in a house when he know the sun is shining.

"Well?" Frank said.

I looked at him, but I didn't answer him. I didn't know what he was talking about.

"Do you think they had to tree him?"

"Not if he treed them," I said.

"Don't underestimate J. W.," Frank said. "Not the way he went out of here with blood in his eyes."

I nodded my head.

"I see you have little confidence in J. W.," Frank said. "Don't you think he's tough?"

"Yes sir," I said. "He's real tough."

"Sure, he's tough," Frank said. "I'll bet you you couldn't find a man anywhere tougher than J. W."

I passed my hand over my mouth to keep from laughing. All the time, 'Malia was over there sewing and humming her church song to herself.

"Five to one, J. W. brings him in," Frank said.

"Sure," I thought. "Sure. But that's not the reason you put on that white shirt and them gray pants."

9: Then we heard it—that yellow gal saying, "Lord, don't tell me I got to start all over again." Then it was quiet for about a second before somebody knocked on the door loud and quick. The kind of loudness and quickness that said, "If you don't hurry up and tell me come in, I'm coming in, anyway."

"Come in," 'Malia said.

But J. W. was already in. In, walking fast, breathing hard. His white shirt was soaking wet. From the collar of the shirt to the cuff of his pants, his clothes was covered with stickers, cuckleburrs, beggar-lice, tar vine leaves, corn silk, and any other grass seed in the field you cared to name. He had to go by me to get to Frank, and I saw how his face was all cut up. The cuts was too thin to come from a knife or a razor, so I figured they had been made by corn leaves and cane leaves.

"He's crazy," J. W. said, even while he was still walking. J. W. wasn't walking the way you walk in a room; he took the long strides you took in the road—like you was trying to make

194

it home before the rain caught you. "There's no doubt—I'm fully convinced he's crazy. Crazy, crazy, crazy. I mean absolutely crazy. Pure-de crazy." He stopped in front of the chair where Frank was sitting. "Yes sir, Mr. Frank, he's crazy." He turned to 'Malia who was sitting by the lamp looking at him. 'Malia wasn't looking at him like she was mad at him for going after Copper, and then coming back calling Copper crazy; she looked at him like she felt pity for him. Pity because she could see that no matter what had happened in the quarters or back in the fields, J. W. had got the worse of it. "Don't mean to say nothing 'gainst your kin at all, Miss Amalia," he said. "Done knowed you all my life, done respected you all my life. But"—he turned to Frank—"that boy crazy. No concern for human beings at all. They don't mean no more to him than a dog or a snake. Not even a good dog, not even a good one. Crazy. Crazy." He jerked his head toward 'Malia again. "I'm sorry, Miss Amalia." Then he jerked his head back toward Frank. "But he crazy, Mr. Frank."

J. W. stopped talking long enough to draw breath and swallow, and all that time Frank was looking at him like he wasn't surprised at all. Looking at him like he had figured that this might happen—like he had already told himself what he had to do if it did happen. That's why he had put on the starched white shirt and the gray pants.

"Crazy 's he can be," J. W. started right where he had left off. "No concern for human beings at all. *"Now*, guess what he done done?"

Frank squinted up at J. W. and shook his head a little, to show him he didn't have the least idea what had happened.

"Nearly 'bout killed half of them boys you sunt me with," J. W. said.

"But he didn't get you?" Frank said, squinting up at him and passing his fingers lightly over his chest.

"Sir? No sir. Only 'cause I was standing a little to the side," J. W. said. "But you ought to see what he did Pool-Doo and Crowley."

"Pool-Doo and Crowley?" Frank said. "What did he do Pool-Doo and Crowley, made them tickle each other half to death?"

"Sir? No sir. It wasn't no tickling—no sir. He just cracked both of them side the head with that little scy' blade handle. I mean hard as he could, Mr. Frank. Hard as he possibly could."

"Where did he got a scythe blade handle from?" Frank asked.

"I don't know, Mr. Frank, but he had it. A brand new one—like it hadn't left the store, yet. Could still see the label."

"You saw the label, but you didn't get close enough for him to crack you side the head?"

"Sir? No sir. I was standing to the side. And guess what he did poor Simon? I'm sure you have no idea what he did that poor boy."

While Frank was trying to guess what Copper did Simon, J. W. wiped the sweat from his face and caught two or three quick breaths of air.

"What did he do Simon?" Frank asked.

"Sir? What he did? He made that poor boy jump in a ditch—a ditch full of yellow jackets—yellow jackets, Mr. Frank."

"I suppose Simon jumped out again?"

"Yes sir. Yes sir. Poor boy. All stung up, all stung up."

Frank passed his hand lightly over his chest again.

"Go on," he said.

"I don't know what happened to Cadilac and Grease."

"Cadilac and Grease?" Frank said.

"Yes sir. Last thing I seen, they was headed toward the

swamps running and hollering. I don't know if they got lost back there or if they fell in the bayou and drowned. The way they was running, they wasn't looking too close where they was going."

J. W. had been talking fast, and now he had to wipe his face and catch his breath again. While Frank was waiting for J. W. to go on, Frank passed his fingers over his chest. He didn't rub hard, just lightly—like even those little light touches was enough to keep his heart beating.

"I honestly think that boy's crazy, Mr. Frank," J. W. started again. "I swear, I honestly do. 'Cause a sane person wouldn't dare act like that—not a sane one." He looked at 'Malia sadly. He was sorry for her for having a crazy nephew on her hands. He turned to Frank again. "Back there checking on everything. Oak trees, pecan trees, berry bushes. Even caught him counting the joints in a stalk of cane."

"Did he look at the cotton?" Frank said.

"Sir? Yes sir. That too."

"Corn?"

"Sir? Corn too. Everything. Everything you can name, he looked at it. Checking them and writing them down in that little tablet. Last thing I seen, he was shelling a yer of corn in his hand and tasting the grains."

Frank sat back in the chair and squinted up at J. W. a long time. J. W. wiped the sweat from his face again. He was still breathing pretty hard; I could see the back of his shoulders going up and down.

"How did you get that shirt so wet—you stopped for a swim before you got back here?" Frank asked.

"Sir? No sir. Just running full speed," J. W. said. " 'Cross cane rows, corn rows, cotton rows—jumping ditches—to tell you what happened."

"All right, you told me; you can leave."

"Yes sir," J. W. said, turning away. Then he stopped and

looked at Frank again. "Yes sir, he told me to tell you, 'When a General ain't got no more army, ain't but one thing for him to do.' "

Frank nodded. "Did he say where he would be?"

"No sir. He just said, 'When a General ain't got no more army, ain't but one thing for him to do.' "

"Go on," Frank said. "Wait. Go back in the field and round up the rest of those worthless niggers; bring them up here so that gal can look after them."

"Yes sir," J. W. said. "Thank you, sir. I'm sure they'll 'preciate that."

J. W. went out, wiping his face and walking fast. Not the way you walk out of a room—the way you walk down the road when you was trying to get home before the rain caught you.

"Felix?" Frank said.

"Yes sir?" I said, getting up from the chair.

"Go back in the quarters and get me everything that can walk or crawl."

"That's about it," I said. "Unless you mean Aunt Jude, Aunt Johnson, and the rest of them. But being in their seventies and eighties and can't back-paddle fast as J. W., I wouldn't want send them on Copper. Not the way he's swinging that little scy' blade handle."

"How about dogs?" Frank said.

"Few of them down there, but putting them all together, I doubt if they'd 'mount to one good one," I said. "And the way Copper's swinging that little scy' blade handle, you'll need at least six or seven. Now, the Cajuns there got some good ones. I'm sure they wouldn't mind lending them to you. We ain't had a good lynching in a long time; they probably wouldn't mind going themself to get him."

"You through, Felix?"

"Yes sir."

"How long do you think they'll let him live if I let him force his way through that front door? Have you thought about that?"

"Can't you let him slip in tonight sometime?"

"Slip in?" Frank said. "Don't you know slipping in to him is the same as coming in through the back?"

I nodded. "I reckon so."

"Even if they didn't lynch him, I wouldn't let him come in through that front door," Frank said. "Neither him, nor you, nor her over there. And to me she is only the second woman I've had the good fortune of knowing whom I can call a lady. But she happens to be black, Felix, and because she's black she'll never enter this house through that door. Not while I'm alive. Because, you see, Felix, I didn't write the rules. I came and found them, and I shall die and leave them. They will be changed, of course; they will be changed, and soon, I hope. But I will not be the one to change them."

He turned to look at 'Malia.

"You crying over there, Amalia?" he asked her.

She shook her head, but she wouldn't look up.

"Yes," Frank said. "If he won't come here, then I must go there. I need some fresh air. I've been in here too long."

"Mr. Frank," 'Malia said, getting up and coming to him. "Don't go down there fooling with Copper. If anybody must go, let me go again."

"No, you stay here," Frank said. "It's me he wants. Can't you see it's me?"

"Don't go down there, Mr. Frank," 'Malia said. "Please, don't go down there."

"I must go, Amalia," Frank said. "I can't let Copper in here."

"And your heart?" she said. She was crying; the water had run down her face to her chin.

Frank stood there looking down at her.

"Poor Amalia," he said. "We all hurt you, don't we, Amalia? Don't worry, I'll be careful. He won't kill me that easily." He turned to me. "I'll have to get my cane and my coat. You must be properly dressed when meeting a General. Meet me in the back; we'll go in the car. You'll have to drive, Felix."

He went out. I put my arm round 'Malia's shoulders and led her back to the chair. She sat there crying. I tried to talk to her, but she was crying too much to answer me.

I left the room, thinking, "Poor woman, poor woman." If it wasn't one of them hurting her, it was the other. Walter did it when he messed up with her niece; the gal did it when she took the boy North; and here was the boy back, hurting her just like his mon and his paw had done before.

10: By the time I had backed the car from under the house, Frank had come down the back stairs. He looked even sicker and weaker. I'm sure if he wasn't using that walking cane he wouldn't 'a' been able to stay on his feet. I held the door open to let him get in the car. Then after he had set himself good, I shut the door and went and got in on the driver's side. We had to drive under the trees to reach the gate. Frank looked out of the window at the trees. It had been a long time since he had been out of that house.

"Felix, why didn't they bring Copper in?" he asked, turning to me. "They didn't want to?"

"They couldn't, Mr. Frank."

"Why? Because he's a Laurent?"

"No sir, that's not it. They couldn't 'a' brought back anybody who didn't want to come."

"Why?" he asked.

"Because it's not like it used to be, Mr. Frank. They not

scared of you like they was scared of Mr. Walter. They knowed you wasn't going to do them anything. They knowed Mr. Walter would 'a' half killed them, and they would 'a' done anything in the world before they came back there empty-handed."

"So it's fear that makes them move?"

"No sir, not exactly. Fear make them move when that's all they ever knowed. But when you lose the power of the rod, of the gun, they ain't got nothing to fear no more."

"I see; they fear the other man who picks up the rod or the gun."

"Yes sir, that's who they fear then."

"Do you think the time might come when they would join up with Copper against me?"

"That I don't know, Mr. Frank."

"Would you, Felix?"

"Well, for one thing, I'm old, Mr. Frank. I don't have too much time left to be joining up with anybody. Another thing, I don't believe in joining up with anybody from fear; I do what I do from respect."

"Do you respect what Copper's doing?"

"Well, I look at it this way: I don't like to see him hurting his aunt like he's doing. But I don't know if I wouldn't slap a few of them up side the head, too, if they came for me like they went for him."

"Then you don't think it's wrong what he's doing?"

"Like I said, Mr. Frank, I don't like to see what he's doing to his aunt."

"Well, how about what he's doing to me?"

"I don't know if he's doing anything, Mr. Frank, Mr. Walter wouldn't 'a' done."

"Walter would have done it," Frank said. "But not Copper's mon. And there is the difference, Felix. And that's why it's wrong."

We was already in the quarters. Far as you could see was nothing but this long road of white dust. It hurt your eyes to look at so much dust, so much whiteness, so much heat rising up from it. It was the hottest part of the day—between one thirty and two—and there wasn't another person anywhere in sight. The tall blood weeds on both sides of the road made the place look even hotter. We was coming up to 'Malia's house. I could see two chairs on the gallery. They wasn't there when I came down the quarters the first time.

"He's waiting for me," Frank said. "Stop the car."

"He made it from the field that quick?"

"He's there," Frank said. "Stop."

I stopped and we looked at the house. Copper didn't show up. Just the two chairs on the gallery facing the road. I mashed on the horn, but he still didn't show up.

"Want me to go and knock?" I asked Frank.

"He's there," Frank said.

I mashed on the horn again, and we waited. About a minute later, Copper came to the door. He had taken off his shirt, and he had a white towel hanging over his shoulder. Me and Frank both looked at him a long time.

"He doesn't look much like a General from here," Frank said. "But I suppose no General looks like a General with his shirt off." He twisted his mouth a little to the side, then he nodded his head and grunted. "Yes, he does look like Walter. Yes."

"Come here, Copper," I called.

He came a little farther out on the gallery, then he stopped again. He just wanted to make sure who was out there.

"You don't think he's coming down those steps, do you?" Frank said.

"Copper? Come here," I said.

"Save your breath," Frank said.

He mashed on the door handle and got out before I could get out and help him. I jumped out on my side and opened the gate. The tall, sick, white man went in the yard with his head high. Copper stood there wide-legged, with his chest out, with his hands on his hips, and watched Frank come up the steps. Frank stood before Copper, leaning on the cane and breathing hard. A few drops of sweat had already settled on his forehead. It had taken everything out of him to come up those steps.

"Uncle," Copper said. They stood face to face. They was about the same height—maybe Frank was a little taller. "I don't see my aunt," Copper said.

"I made her stay at the house," Frank said.

"You *made* her stay there, huh?"

Then they just stood there looking at each other. You could see Frank wanted to raise that cane and bring it down on Copper's head or his shoulder. But he didn't have the strength to do it. And even if he had, he probably wouldn't 'a' done it then. What he wanted more than anything else, now, was to find out what Copper was doing here.

Copper had said "Uncle" to Frank just like he would 'a' said "Aunt" to 'Malia. It was like he had been calling him that all his life. He was no more scared of Frank than Frank was scared of him. They was both Laurents. A Laurent wasn't supposed to be scared of any man.

"Please sit down, Uncle," Copper said.

Frank still wouldn't move for a while. You didn't ask a Laurent to sit down, just like you didn't ask him to stand up or shut his mouth. The Laurents moved when they wanted to move. But once he had gone to that chair, I could see how glad he was to sit down. To get dressed, to come down the stairs at the big house, to come up the steps here had taken everything out of him.

"I'm sorry you found me like this," Copper said, "but I

had just come in from the field. Would you like a glass of ice water while I change clothes? I also have some lemonade there."

"Water is fine," Frank said.

"Get some water," Copper said to me.

He didn't talk to me like he was talking to a' old man, he spoke to me like he was speaking to a slave. I went back in the kitchen to get the water. On my way back I met him coming in the house. I had to step out his way to keep him from walking over me. I'm sure he didn't see me at all. He was looking at something far away, or like he was listening to something far away. If you've seen people walking in their sleep, that's the way he looked.

I went out on the gallery and handed Frank the glass of water.

"I used to come here when I was a young man," he said, after he had drunk. "I used to sit on those steps. That mulberry tree there is old as I am."

"I remember it from 'way back," I said.

"I never thought I'd ever sit here again," Frank said.

He looked at all the things round him, then he finished drinking the water and handed me the glass.

Copper came back on the gallery a few minutes later. He had put on more khakis. Not the cheap khakis people wore in the field—the good kind officers wore in the Army. He had on another pair of shoes. They shined better than the other pair did this morning. He stood in the door a second before he came over to the bannister and sat down. He sat a little to the right of Frank's chair. I stood near the steps and leaned back against the post.

"You have two chairs there," Frank said. "Aren't you going to sit down?"

"The bannister is perfectly all right," Copper said. "The other chair was for my aunt."

"Well, she's at the house," Frank said.

"Yes, you *made* her stay there," Copper said.

"Can Felix sit in the chair?"

"Would you have let Felix sit on the gallery at your house?"

"He was sitting in my living room just before we came here," Frank said.

"I'm sure he was," Copper said. "Was he sitting in the living room yesterday? Will he sit there tomorrow?"

"No," Frank said.

They looked at each other like two rams locking horns. But Frank wasn't mad with Copper now; he was just playing round with words. He had caught his breath and had even gotten a little color in his face.

Frank raised the walking cane and tapped the bannister two or three inches away from where Copper was sitting. Copper looked straight at Frank all the time. I said he was looking at Frank, I didn't say he was seeing Frank; because even when he was looking at you, even when he was talking to you, it looked like he was listening to something 'way off.

"What do you want, boy?" Frank asked Copper.

"My birthright," Copper said.

Now, Frank sat 'way back in the chair. He rested one of his arms, his left arm, on the arm of the chair. Then he squinted up at Copper. He had heard Copper quite well, but he didn't believe what he had heard.

"Your what?" he said.

"My birthright," Copper said, looking straight at him.

"That nigger of mine told me he thought you were crazy," Frank said.

Copper didn't say anything, but he never took his eyes off Frank.

"Well?" Frank said.

"What do you think?" Copper said.

"I think he's a good judge of character," Frank said.

Copper raised his hand to his left temple. But I noticed just before he touched his face, his mind drifted away a moment. He didn't rub his temple, he touched it lightly—the way Frank touched at his chest every so often.

"You know anything about the history of this country, boy?" Frank asked him.

"I know a little history," Copper said.

"Then you know because your mon was black you can't claim a damn thing. Not only birthright, you can't even claim a cat."

"Maybe I can't claim my birthright today," Copper said. "But I'll claim it tomorrow."

"Tomorrow?" Frank said.

Copper nodded. "Tomorrow."

"How do you expect to perform that miracle?"

"No miracle, Uncle," Copper said. "My men and I'll just do it."

"Your men?"

"My men."

"And who are these men, Copper?"

"The name is Christian, Uncle," Copper said. "Laurent. Christian Laurent. General Christian Laurent."

"Who are these men, General?" Frank said.

"All those who've been treated as I've been treated," Copper said. (When Copper was talking to you, he wasn't seeing you, he was seeing something 'way off.) He touched at his temple again. Frank watched his hand go up and come back down. "There are many just like me. So many just like me," he said.

Frank let his eyes shift from Copper's face down to his clothes. His khakis was starched and ironed; his shoes shined like new tin.

"Copper," Frank said, leaning closer toward him, "you're

insane, aren't you, boy? There aren't any men, are there?"

"The name is Christian, Uncle."

"There aren't any men, are there, Christian?"

"Yes and no," Copper said. "Spiritually, yes, and they're waiting for me. Physically, in the sense of an organized Army, no."

"How do you know that your imaginary Army will ever materialize, Christian?"

"Just smell the air, Uncle."

Frank looked at Copper a while, like he was letting all this soak in. Then he raised his head and took a deep breath.

"No, I don't smell a thing," he said. He turned to me. "You, Felix?"

I didn't answer him. I didn't believe in getting in kin-folks' squabbles. They always turned against *you* in the end.

"It's there, Uncle," Copper said. "Only a fool, and a damn one at that, can't smell what's in the air."

I looked at Frank and I saw a little color shoot out of his face. He probably would 'a' had another heart attack if any-body else had called him a damn fool; but Copper had said so much already, to hear Copper call him a damn fool didn't shock him too much.

"Any more water in that glass, Felix?" he asked me.

"No sir; I'll get some."

I hurried inside and got the water and hurried back. Frank drank a little and handed me the glass. I moved back against the post.

Frank tapped the bannister with the walking cane and looked up at Copper.

"And you're the General?" he said.

"I am the General," Copper said.

"Suppose I kill this General, which I can do as easily as snapping my fingers, then what?"

"You won't kill this General, or you would have done it

before now, Uncle," Copper said. "And that's a grave mistake, not killing him. But even if you did kill this General, another General would only spring up."

"Not on my place, claiming birthright," Frank said.

"If not on your place claiming birthright, then on somebody else's place claiming birthright," Copper said. "It was not only on your place he was denied his birthright. That's been denied him all over this country."

"I see you have the answers, General," Frank said.

"That's why I am a General, Uncle," Copper said.

Frank squinted up at Copper a second, then he sat back in the chair and sniffed at the air again. Copper raised his left hand and rubbed his finger lightly over his temple. For a second there, his mind drifted away from him again. He might 'a' been listening to something far off.

11: "You know, you almost killed half of my men on this place," Frank said.

Copper had been looking at Frank, but he had been thinking about something else. Frank woke him out of a dream.

"Men?" he said.

Frank nodded. "Men."

"Since when have you started calling them men, Uncle?" Copper asked.

Frank didn't answer him then; he squinted up at Copper a while. "So that's why you did it?" he said.

"When they act like men, I'll treat them like men," Copper said. "When they let you make them act like animals, then I'll treat them like animals."

"I see," Frank said. "You're going to change it all. You, one, are going to change what's been drilled into their brains the past three hundred years? You, one?"

"That's my intention," Copper said.

"Using chains and sticks?" Frank asked him.

Copper didn't answer him then; he let Frank think about what he had said. Then I saw this slow grin coming on Copper's face.

"Did you say chains and sticks—Uncle?" he said.

"Yes."

"I thought you said chains and sticks," Copper said. "I thought I heard you right."

He didn't go on for a while; he wanted Frank to think some more.

"Those are your creations, Uncle—the chains and sticks. You created them four hundred years ago, and you're still using them up to this day. You created them. But they were only a fraction of your barbarity—Uncle. You used the rope and the tree to hang him. You used the knife to castrate him while he struggled with the rope to catch his breath. You used fire to make him squirm even more, because the hanging and the castration still wasn't enough amusement for you. Then you used something else—another creation of yours— that thing *you* called law. It was written by you for you and your kind, and any man who was not of your kind had to break it sooner or later. . . . I only used a fraction of your creations. You have imbedded the stick and the chain in their minds for so long, they can't hear anything else. I needed it to get their attention. I think I have it now—and I won't have to use it any more. From now on I'll use the simplest words. Simple words, Uncle; a thing you thought they would never understand."

All the time Copper was talking, he kept his voice calm and even. But it was a strain for him, just like it was a strain for him to sit in one place. I don't mean he was squirming round on the bannister; but you had the feeling he might 'a' jumped up from there any moment. I noticed once how his mind drifted away, stayed away for a while, before it came back again.

Frank put the palm of his hand on the end of the walking cane and pressed it against the floor. If this was out in the yard, the point of the cane would 'a' made a slight hole in the ground. He squinted up at Copper. He was like a lawyer in the courtroom. Maybe the other lawyer had said something that was the truth, and maybe he felt like telling the lawyer he had said some true things, but that wasn't going to change his feelings at all.

"That nigger of mine told me you had a notebook," he said. "What were you doing, mapping out plans for battle?"

"Just making a few notes on the place," Copper said. He could see Frank was trying to play with him, but he didn't mind this at all. Because everything he said, himself, he meant it. "The condition of the houses, the crops, the fertility of the land," he said.

"And what do you think of the place?" Frank said, looking at the little mulberry tree, not at Copper.

But when he did that he forgot Copper was a Laurent. He thought Copper was going to answer him like I would 'a' answered him, or like one of his sharecroppers had to answer him. Copper just sat there, looking down at him in that extra calm way he possessed. Frank kept on looking at the tree, waiting. But when the answer didn't come, I could see his eyes shifting down the tree near the ground. He wasn't seeing the tree now, he was waiting for something, a sound or something, to make him face Copper again. Since he had turned his head from Copper, he needed something to make him turn back. That was supposed to be my job, I reckoned, but I wasn't getting in it. Let him get out of it the best way he could. After a while, he looked back on his own.

"The land has been wasted and is still being wasted, but it's not beyond saving," Copper said. If he took what Frank had done as a' insult, he wasn't showing it. "As for the houses, they'll have to be torn down and built from the ground up," he said.

"Corn?" Frank said. "That nigger told me you ate a few grains of my corn back there."

"I did," Copper said. "Most of it is bad. Not terrible, but it could be better."

"Cotton?" Frank said.

"It can be improved."

"Cane?" Frank said.

"Same as the cotton and corn."

"Hay?" Frank said.

"Yes."

"Berries?" he said.

Copper nodded.

"Did you get into the swamps?"

"I would have," Copper said. "But I was being continually interrupted."

"J. W. and Little Boy?" Frank said.

"Was that their names?"

"Yes," Frank said, "that was their names."

"They didn't introduce themselves," Copper said.

Frank poked the cane in the floor again. If this was out in the yard, it would 'a' made a hole in the ground 'a' inch deep. He squinted up at Copper.

"When did this birthright notion come into your head?" he asked.

You could see in Copper's face how his mind went and came back. He was looking at Frank one second and seeing him; then the next second he was seeing something 'way off.

"I always knew who my father was," he said, keeping his voice level. Now his mind had drifted 'way again. He made a painful frown, and I saw the left side of his face trembling.

"But I knew I couldn't say a thing about it. It would have gotten me in trouble, and probably gotten my mother in more trouble. Then one day in the field we were picking up potatoes. I had gone to the bayou to get some water out of the barrel. When I came back to the row where my mother and I were working, she wasn't there. I asked where she was, and a woman—I forget who she was—started laughing at me. I walked away crying, looking for my mother. I found them in another patch of ground, Walter Laurent on top of her. They didn't see me, but that night I told her one day I was going to kill him. That's why we moved from here. Her, her husband and me. Her husband's name was the name I carried up until recently."

Copper raised his hand up to his face to touch both of his temples. I could see him frowning behind his hand.

"Two years after we left here, my mother died," Copper went on. He was looking at Frank, but he wasn't seeing him; he was seeing past Frank. Like he was talking to Frank, but at the same time listening to another voice. "My suppose-to-be father, who had been too nutless to say I wasn't his while we lived in the South, kicked me out of the house before my mother was cold in her grave. He was not going to support any white man's child. He was tired supporting a white man's child. I was fourteen years old then. A fourteen-year-old black child out on his own. Not a soul in the world to turn to, not one."

He stopped and looked down at Frank again. Frank wasn't looking at him now; he had folded his hands over the end of the walking cane and he had propped his chin on his hands. Even when Copper had quit talking, even when he knowed Copper was looking down at him, he kept his head bowed.

"For the last ten years I've been everywhere," Copper said, looking at the trees over in the other yard—looking at them, but not seeing one of them. "I've seen a little bit of everything in this world, but suffering more than anything else. There're millions just like me. Maybe not my color, but without homes, without birthrights, just like me. And who is to blame?" he said, looking down at Frank. "Men like my father. Men like Walter Laurent."

Frank raised his eyes to look at him. He didn't move his chin from his hands. He looked at Copper long and carefully, then he looked down again.

"Rapists," Copper said. "Murderers, plunderers—and they hide behind the law. The law they created themselves."

He got up from the bannister and went to the other end of the gallery. I saw him looking across the yard toward the big house. I saw him raising both of his hands and pressing them hard against his face.

"The suffering, the suffering, the suffering," he said.

He rubbed his face hard, and just looked at that house a long time. I watched him, but Frank didn't. He kept his head bowed, his chin resting on his hands. He didn't even look up when Copper came back to the bannister.

"I've been in all the cities," Copper said. He was calm again—but he was too calm. "Yes, and I've been in prison. How many times have I heard weeping in those cells. How many times did they make me scrub the blood off the floor. Once, just to show me what it looked like, they made me clean the chair. I found a strain of hair, a long, brown strain of hair. I kept it for a while, then I lost it. It didn't matter. I didn't need a strain of hair to remind me of the horror I had seen." He stopped and looked down at his uncle. "But why?" he said. "Why? What have we done? We didn't even ask to be born. I, myself, was conceived in a ditch. . . . And now . . . day and night . . . day and night . . . day and night . . ." He stopped. He had to wait till his mind came back again. "Why these washed-out eyes, these distorted minds, these nonfunc-

213

tioning brains? Why do I see the faces and hear the cries still? Not powerful cries—little whimpers, like mice in a trap. In a crowd or alone, their cries are with me." He threw his head back. "Clinging to me, won't let me be free," he screamed. He stopped again; he pressed both of his hands against the sides of his face. He was looking down at his uncle. He was seeing him, he wasn't seeing him. For a second, there, he felt sorry for his uncle; looked like he wanted to cry. He made a deep frown; his mouth trembled, the way a man trembles just before he cries. But, then, he remembered he was a General, and the same General who couldn't go through that back door couldn't cry either. "I used to pray once," he said. He was calm again—too calm. "I used to pray and pray and pray. But the same God I was praying to was created by the same ones I was praying against. And Gods only listen to the people who create them. So I quit my praying—there would have to be another way. I remembered that I had a father who had property, and I remembered that I was his oldest son. I would take that property—my share of that property— and I would share it with those others who were like me."

He stopped and looked down at the floor. He looked very tired. Sweat had broke out on his face, and even his starched khaki shirt was wet round the armpit. Frank raised his head slowly and looked at Copper.

"So you made yourself a General?" he said.

"The world made me a General," Copper said. "But you wouldn't know what that means, would you?"

"Hardly," Frank said. "I've had it easy all my life. I've never heard anyone cry; I've never seen any washed-out eyes. Never seen anybody sick."

"No, not the way I have," Copper said. "Because you've always been in a position to give them a dime. Dimes clear all conscience."

Frank sat back in the chair—with his walking cane on the

right side of the chair, with his arm resting on one of the chair arms, with his legs stretched out, with his head back— looking up at Copper.

"J. W. is a good judge of character," he said. "You are insane, boy. As insane as anyone has ever been. To think you can carry the burden of this world on your shoulders is not an original idea. That idea is old as man's idea of justice—prob- ably as old as man himself. Since the beginning of civilization he has tried to do exactly what you want to do, but since it was as insane then as it is now, he has failed. My brother, your father, was wrong. Not only with your mother, but with many other women—white and black alike. White and black men he also destroyed. Destroyed them physically, destroyed them mentally. I, myself, have suffered from his errors as much as you, as much as any other man has, but I—"

"You have not suffered," Copper said.

"Shut up when I'm talking," Frank said. "I listened to you."

Copper slid away from the bannister real slowly and stood right in front of the chair. For a moment I thought he was going to jerk Frank out of there and slam him against the wall. Because, if he had done it, it wouldn't 'a' surprised me at all. Frank looked up at Copper when he stood up. He wasn't scared of Copper; he didn't even get a tighter grip on the cane. He challenged Copper a while, just looking at him, then he nodded. I supposed he re'lized he wasn't being a gentleman.

"Don't talk to me like that ever again," Copper said. "I'm not one of your niggers running round in the quarters. I'm not one your Cajun sharecroppers. Whether you like it or not, I'm a Laurent. I'm a Laurent, Uncle, and you better remember it."

"My apologies—Nephew," Frank said. "Now, shall I go on?"

Copper didn't say any more, but he didn't sit down either. He just stood there, looking down at Frank.

"I was saying I've suffered as much as you've suffered," Frank said. "He's destroyed your mind, he's destroyed my body. I don't know how much more time I have. Maybe a year, maybe a month, maybe only another day. But as long as I'm here I'm going to do all I can to make up for what he did to these here in the quarters. I'm going to give them shelter and food, medicine when they're sick, a place to worship God. When they die, I'm going to give them a little plot of ground in which to be buried." He sat up a little in the chair and squinted up at Copper. "General Christian Laurent, I'm going to defend this place with all my strength. I'm going to defend it with my dying breath—to keep it exactly as it is. And if you come back here again, alone or with your Army, before the law of the land has been changed to give you those 'birthrights' you've been talking so much about, I would shoot you down the same as I would a mad dog. After I'm dead, laws won't matter to me. You and Greta Jean can fight over this piece of rot as long as you both live. But as long as I can draw breath, it stays as it is. I did not write these rules and laws you've been talking about; I came here and found them just as you did. And neither one of us is going to change them, not singly. Now, those are my last words to you. You can stay here as long as you think it's possible to stay without causing trouble. If you can't live by those rules, then you better get the hell away from here now."

Copper stood there a long time after Frank had finished talking. He even narrowed his eyes and looked down at Frank the way all the Laurents did.

"Are you finished, Uncle?" he said.

Frank didn't answer him. He was looking down the quarters now.

"I'll leave, Uncle," Copper said. "Not because you are

frightening me—that's impossible; nothing frightens me any more. I'll leave because I only came this time to look around. But I'll be back. We'll be back, Uncle. And I'll take my share. I won't beg for it, I won't ask for it; I'll take it. I'll take it or I'll bathe this whole plantation in blood."

He stopped and looked down at Frank. Frank was still looking down the quarters.

"Your days are over, Uncle," he said. "It's my time now. And I won't let a thing in the world get in my way. Nothing . . .

"Shall I help you back to the car?"

"I have Felix there," Frank said, without looking at him.

"Then I'll say good day," Copper said. "Tell my aunt I've gone. But tell her I'll come back. And tell her when I do, she'll never have to go through your back door ever again."

He bowed and went inside—walking fast the way soldiers walk.

Just Like A Tree

JUST LIKE A TREE

I shall not;
  I shall not be moved.
I shall not;
  I shall not be moved.
Just like a tree that's
planted 'side the water.
    Oh, I shall not be moved.

I made my home in glory;
  I shall not be moved.
Made my home in glory;
  I shall not be moved.
Just like a tree that's
planted 'side the water.
    Oh, I shall not be moved.
      (from an old Negro spiritual)

Chuckkie

Pa hit him on the back and he jeck in them chains like he pulling, but ever'body in the wagon know he ain't, and Pa hit him on the back again. He jeck again like he pulling, but even Big Red know he ain't doing a thing.

"That's why I'm go'n get a horse," Pa say. "He'll kill that other mule. Get up there, Mr. Bascom."

"Oh, let him alone," Gran'mon say. "How would you like it if you was pulling a wagon in all that mud?"

Pa don't answer Gran'mon; he just hit Mr. Bascom on the back again.

"That's right, kill him," Gran'mon say. "See where you get mo' money to buy another one."

"Get up there, Mr. Bascom," Pa say.

"You hear me talking to you, Emile?" Gran'mon say. "You want me hit you with something?"

"Ma, he ain't pulling," Pa say.

"Leave him alone," Gran'mon say.

Pa shake the lines little bit, but Mr. Bascom don't even feel it, and you can see he letting Big Red do all the pulling again. Pa say something kind o' low to hisself, and I can't make out what it is.

I low' my head little bit, 'cause that wind and fine rain was hitting me in the face, and I can feel Mama pressing close to me to keep me warm. She sitting on one side o' me and Pa sitting on the other side o' me, and Gran'mon in the back o' me in her setting chair. Pa didn't want bring the setting chair, telling Gran'mon there was two boards in that wagon already and she could sit on one of 'em all by herself if she wanted to, but Gran'mon say she was taking her setting chair with her if Pa liked it or not. She say she didn't ride in no wagon on nobody board, and if Pa liked it or not, that setting chair was going.

"Let her take her setting chair," Mama say. "What's wrong with taking her setting chair."

"Ehhh, Lord," Pa say, and picked up the setting chair and took it out to the wagon. "I guess I'll have to bring it back in the house, too, when we come back from there."

Gran'mon went and clambed in the wagon and moved her setting chair back little bit and sat down and folded her arms, waiting for us to get in, too. I got in and knelt down 'side her, but Mama told me to come up there and sit on the board 'side her and Pa so I could stay warm. Soon 's I sat down, Pa hit Mr. Bascom on the back, saying what a trifling thing Mr. Bascom was, and soon 's he got some mo' money he was getting rid o' Mr. Bascom and getting him a horse.

I raise my head to look see how far we is.

"That's it, yonder," I say.

"Stop pointing," Mama say, "and keep your hand in your pocket."

"Where?" Gran'mon say, back there in her setting chair.

" 'Cross the ditch, yonder," I say.

"Can't see a thing for this rain," Gran'mon say.

"Can't hardly see it," I say. "But you can see the light little bit. That chinaball tree standing in the way."

"Poor soul," Gran'mon say. "Poor soul."

I know Gran'mon was go'n say "poor soul, poor soul," 'cause she had been saying "poor soul, poor soul," ever since she heard Aunt Fe was go'n leave from back there.

Emile

Darn cane crop to finish getting in and only a mule and a half to do it. If I had my way I'd take that shotgun and a load o' buckshots and—but what's the use.

"Get up, Mr. Bascom—please," I say to that little dried-up, long-eared, tobacco-color thing. "Please, come up. Do your share for God sake—if you don't mind. I know it's hard pulling in all that mud, but if you don't do your share, then Big Red'll have to do his and yours, too. So, please, if it ain't asking you too much to—"

"Oh, Emile, shut up," Leola say.

"I can't hit him," I say, "or Mama back there'll hit me. So I have to talk to him. Please, Mr. Bascom, if you don't mind it. For my sake. No, not for mine; for God sake. No, not even for His'n; for Big Red sake. A fellow mule just like yourself is. Please, come up."

"Now, you hear that boy blaspheming God right in front o' me there," Mama say. "Ehhh, Lord—just keep it up. All this bad weather there like this whole world coming apart—a clap o' thunder come there and knock the fool out you. Just keep it up."

Maybe she right, and I stop. I look at Mr. Bascom there doing nothing, and I just give up. That mule know long 's Mama's alive he go'n do just what he want to do. He know when Papa was dying he told Mama to look after him, and he know no matter what he do, no matter what he don't do, Mama ain't go'n never let me do him anything. Sometimes I even feel Mama care mo' for Mr. Bascom 'an she care for me her own son.

We come up to the gate and I pull back on the lines.

"Whoa up, Big Red," I say. "You don't have to stop, Mr. Bascom. You never started."

I can feel Mama looking at me back there in that setting chair, but she don't say nothing.

"Here," I say to Chuckkie.

He take the lines and I jump down on the ground to open the old beat-up gate. I see Etienne's horse in the yard, and I see Chris new red tractor 'side the house, shining in the rain. When Mama die, I say to myself, Mr. Bascom, you going. Ever'body getting tractors and horses and I'm still stuck with you. You going, brother.

"Can you make it through?" I ask Chuckkie. "That gate ain't too wide."

"I can do it," he say.

"Be sure to make Mr. Bascom pull," I say.

"Emile, you better get back up here and drive 'em through," Leola say. "Chuckkie might break up that wagon."

"No, let him stay down there and give orders," Mama say, back there in that setting chair.

"He can do it," I say. "Come on, Chuckkie boy."

"Come up, here, mule," Chuckkie say.

And soon 's he say that, Big Red make a lunge for the yard, and Mr. Bascom don't even move, and 'fore I can bat my eyes I hear *pow-wow; sagg-sagg; pow-wow*. But above all that noise, Leola up there screaming her head off. And Mama —not a word; just sitting in that chair, looking at me with her arms still folded.

"Pull Big Red," I say. "Pull Big Red, Chuckkie."

Poor little Chuckkie up there pulling so hard till one of his little arms straight out in back; and Big Red throwing his shoulders and ever'thing else in it, and Mr. Bascom just walking there just 's loose and free, like he's suppose to be there just for his good looks. I move out the way just in time to let the wagon go by me, pulling half o' the fence in the yard behind it. I glance up again, and there's Leola still hollering and trying to jump out, but Mama not saying a word—just sitting there in that setting chair with her arms still folded.

"Whoa," I hear little Chuckkie saying. "Whoa up, now."

Somebody open the door and a bunch o' people come out on the gallery.

"What the world—?" Etienne say. "Thought the whole place was coming to pieces there."

"Chuckkie had a little trouble coming in the yard," I say.

"Goodness," Etienne say. "Anybody hurt?"

Mama just sit there about ten seconds, then she say something to herself and start clambing out the wagon.

"Let me help you there, Aunt Lou," Etienne say, coming down the steps."

"I can make it," Mama say. When she get on the ground she look up at Chuckkie. "Hand me my chair there, boy."

Poor little Chuckkie, up there with the lines in one hand, get the chair and hold it to the side, and Etienne catch it just 'fore it hit the ground. Mama start looking at me again, and it look like for at least a' hour she stand there looking at nobody but me. Then she say, "Ehhh, Lord," like that again, and go inside with Leola and the rest o' the people.

I look back at half o' the fence laying there in the yard, and I jump back on the wagon and guide the mules to the side o' the house. After unhitching 'em and tying 'em to the wheels, I look at Chris pretty red tractor again, and me and Chuckkie go inside: I make sure he kick all that mud off his shoes 'fore he go in the house.

Leola

Sitting over there by that fireplace, trying to look joyful when ever'body there know she ain't. But she trying, you know; smiling and bowing when people say something to her. How can she be joyful, I ask you; how can she be? Poor thing, she been here all her life—or the most of it, let's say. 'Fore they moved in this house, they lived in one back in the woods 'bout a mile from here. But for the past twenty-five or thirty years, she been right in this one house. I know ever since I been big enough to know people I been seeing her right here.

Aunt Fe, Aunt Fe, Aunt Fe, Aunt Fe; the name's been 'mongst us just like us own family name. Just like the name o' God. Like the name of town—the city. Aunt Fe, Aunt Fe, Aunt Fe, Aunt Fe.

Poor old thing; how many times I done come here and washed clothes for her when she couldn't do it herself. How many times I done hoed in that garden, ironed her clothes, wrung a chicken neck for her. You count the days in the year and you'll be pretty close. And I didn't mind it a bit. No, I didn't mind it a bit. She there trying to pay me. Proud— Lord, talking 'bout pride. "Here." "No, Aunt Fe; no." "Here, here; you got a child there, you can use it." "No, Aunt Fe. No. No. What would Mama think if she knowed I took money from you? Aunt Fe, Mama would never forgive me. No. I love doing these thing for you. I just wish I could do more."

And there, now, trying to make 'tend she don't mind leaving. Ehhh, Lord.

I hear a bunch o' rattling round in the kitchen and I go back there. I see Louise stirring this big pot o' eggnog.

"Louise," I say.

"Leola," she say.

We look at each other and she stir the eggnog again. She know what I'm go'n say next, and she can't even look in my face.

"Louise, I wish there was some other way."

"There's no other way," she say.

"Louise, moving her from here's like moving a tree you been used to in your front yard all your life."

"What else can I do?"

"Oh, Louise, Louise."

"Nothing else but that."

"Louise, what people go'n do without her here?"

She stir the eggnog and don't answer.

"Louise, us'll take her in with us."

"You all no kin to Auntie. She go with me."

"And us'll never see her again."

She stir the eggnog. Her husband come back in the kitchen and kiss her on the back o' the neck and then look at me and grin. Right from the start I can see I ain't go'n like that nigger.

"Almost ready, honey?" he say.

"Almost."

He go to the safe and get one o' them bottles of whiskey he got in there and come back to the stove.

"No," Louise say. "Everybody don't like whiskey in it. Add the whiskey after you've poured it up."

"Okay, hon."

He kiss her on the back o' the neck again. Still don't like that nigger. Something 'bout him ain't right.

"You one o' the family?" he say.

"Same as one," I say. "And you?"

He don't like the way I say it, and I don't care if he like it or not. He look at me there a second, and then he kiss her on the ear.

"Un-unnn," she say, stirring the pot.

"I love your ear, baby," he say.

"Go in the front room and talk with the people," she say.

He kiss her on the other ear. A nigger do all that front o' public got something to hide. He leave the kitchen. I look at Louise.

"Ain't nothing else I can do," she say.

228

"You sure, Louise? You positive?"

"I'm positive," she say.

The front door open and Emile and Chuckkie come in. A minute later Washington and Adrieu come in, too. Adrieu come back in the kitchen, and I can see she been crying. Aunt Fe is her godmother, you know.

"How you feel, Adrieu?"

"That weather out there," she say.

"Y'all walked?"

"Yes."

"Us here in the wagon. Y'all can go back with us."

"Y'all the one tore the fence down?" she ask.

"Yes, I guess so. That brother-in-law o' yours in there letting Chuckkie drive that wagon."

"Well, I don't guess it'll matter too much. Nobody go'n be here, anyhow."

And she start crying again. I take her in my arms and pat her on the shoulder, and I look at Louise stirring the eggnog.

"What I'm go'n do and my nan-nane gone? I love her so much."

"Ever'body love her."

"Since my mama died, she been like my mama."

"Shhh," I say. "Don't let her hear you. Make her grieve. You don't want her grieving, now, do you?"

She sniffs there 'gainst my dress few times.

"Oh, Lord," she say. "Lord, have mercy."

"Shhh," I say. "Shhh. That's what life's 'bout."

"That ain't what life's 'bout," she say. "It ain't fair. This been her home all her life. These the people she know. She don't know them people she going to. It ain't fair."

"Shhh, Adrieu," I say. "Now, you saying things that ain't your business."

She cry there some mo'.

229

"Oh, Lord, Lord," she say.

Louise turn from the stove.

"About ready now," she say, going to the middle door. "James, tell everybody to come back and get some."

James

Let me go on back here and show these country niggers how to have a good time. All they know is talk, talk, talk. Talk so much they make me buggy round here. Damn this weather—wind, rain. Must be a million cracks in this old house.

I go to that old beat-up safe in that corner and get that fifth of Mr. Harper (in the South now; got to say Mister), give the seal one swipe, the stopper one jerk, and head back to that old wood stove. (Man, like, these cats are primitive—goodness. You know what I mean? I mean like wood stoves. Don't mention TV, man, these cats here never heard of that.) I start to dump Mr. Harper in the pot and Baby catches my hand again and say not all of them like it. You ever heard of anything like that? I mean a stud's going to drink eggnog, and he's not going to put whiskey in it. I mean he's going to drink it straight. I mean, you ever heard anything like that? Well, I wasn't pressing none of them on Mr. Harper. I mean, me and Mr. Harper get along too well together for me to go around there pressing.

I hold my cup there and let Baby put a few drops of this egg stuff in it; then I jerk my cup back and let Mr. Harper run a while. Couple of these cats come over (some of them aren't so lame) and set their cups, and I let Mr. Harper run for them. Then this cat says he's got 'nough. I let Mr. Harper run for this other stud, and pretty soon he says, "Hold it. Good." Country cat, you know. "Hold it. Good." Real country cat. So I raise the cup to see what Mr. Harper's doing. He's just right. I raise the cup again. Just right, Mr. Harper; just right.

I go to the door with Mr. Harper under my arm and the cup in my hand and I look into the front room where they all are. I mean, there's about ninety-nine of them in there. Old ones, young ones, little ones, big ones, yellow ones, black ones, brown ones—you name them, brother, and they were there. And what for? Brother, I'll tell you what for. Just because me and Baby are taking this old chick out of these sticks. Well, I'll tell you where I'd be at this moment if I was one of them. With that weather out there like it is, I'd be under about five blankets with some little warm belly pressing against mine. Brother, you can bet your hat I wouldn't be here. Man, listen to that thing out there. You can hear that rain beating on that old house like grains of rice; and that wind coming through them cracks like it does in those old Charlie Chaplin movies. Man, like you know—like *whooo-ee; whooo-ee.* Man, you talking about some weird cats.

I can feel Mr. Harper starting to massage my wig and I bat my eyes twice and look at the old girl over there. She's still sitting in that funny-looking little old rocking chair, and not saying a word to anybody. Just sitting there looking into the fireplace at them two pieces of wood that aren't giving out enough heat to warm a baby, let alone ninety-nine grown people. I mean, you know, like that sleet's falling out there like all get-up-and-go, and them two pieces of wood are lying there just as dead as the rest of these way-out cats.

One of the old cats—I don't know which one he is—Mose, Sam, or something like that—leans over and pokes in the fire a minute; then a little blaze shoots up, and he raises up, too, looking as satisfied as if he'd just sent a rocket into orbit. I mean, these cats are like that. They do these little bitty things, and they feel like they've really done something.

Well, back in these sticks, I guess there just isn't nothing big to do.

I feel Mr. Harper touching my skull now—and I notice this little chick passing by me with these two cups of eggnog. She goes over to the fireplace and gives one to each of these old chicks. The one sitting in that setting chair she brought with her from God knows where, and the other cup to the old chick that Baby and I are going to haul from here sometime tomorrow morning. Wait, man, I mean like, you ever heard of anybody going to somebody else's house with a chair? I mean, wouldn't you call that an insult at the basest point? I mean, now, like tell me what you think of that? I mean—dig— here I am at my pad, and in you come with your own stool. I mean, now, like man, you know. I mean that's an insult at the basest point. I mean, you know . . . you know, like way out. . . .

Mr. Harper, what you trying to do, boy?—I mean, *sir*. (Got to watch myself, I'm in the South. Got to keep watching myself.)

This stud touches me on the shoulder and raise his cup and say, "How 'bout a taste?" I know what the stud's talking about, so I let Mr. Harper run for him. But soon 's I let a drop get in, the stud say, " 'Nough." I mean I let about two drops get in, and already the stud's got enough. Man, I mean, like you know. I mean these studs are 'way out. I mean like 'way back there.

This stud takes a swig of his eggnog and say, "Ahhh." I mean this real down-home way of saying "Ahhhh." I mean, man, like these studs—I notice this little chick passing by me again, and this time she's crying. I mean weeping, you know. And just because this old ninety-nine-year-old chick's packing up and leaving. I mean, you ever heard of anything like that? I mean, here she is pretty as the day is long and crying be- cause Baby and I are hauling this old chick away. Well, I'd like to make her cry. And I can assure you, brother, it wouldn't be from leaving her.

I turn and look at Baby over there by the stove, pouring eggnog in all these cups. I mean, there're about twenty of these cats lined up there. And I bet you not half of them will take Mr. Harper along. Some way-out cats, man. Some way-out cats.

I go up to Baby and kiss her on the back of the neck and give her a little pat where she likes for me to pat her when we're in the bed. She say, "Uh-uh," but I know she likes it anyhow.

Ben O

I back under the bed and touch the slop jar, and I pull back my leg and back somewhere else, and then I get me a good sight on it. I spin my aggie couple times and sight again and then I shoot. I hit it right square in the middle and it go flying over the fireplace. I crawl over there to get it and I see 'em all over there drinking they eggnog and they didn't even offer me and Chuckkie none. I find my marble on the bricks, and I go back and tell Chuckkie they over there drinking eggnog.

"You want some?" I say.

"I want shoot marble," Chuckkie say. "Yo' shot. Shoot up."

"I want some eggnog," I say.

"Shoot up, Ben O," he say. "I'm getting cold staying in one place so long. You feel that draft?"

"Coming from that crack under that bed," I say.

"Where?" Chuckkie say, looking for the crack.

"Over by that bedpost over there," I say.

"This sure's a beat-up old house," Chuckkie say.

"I want me some eggnog," I say.

"Well, you ain't getting none," Gran'mon say, from the fireplace. "It ain't good for you."

"I can drink eggnog," I say. "How come it ain't good for me? It ain't nothing but eggs and milk. I eat chicken, don't I? I eat beef, don't I?"

Gran'mon don't say nothing.

"I want me some eggnog," I say.

Gran'mon still don't say no more. Nobody else don't say nothing, neither.

"I want me some eggnog," I say.

"You go'n get a eggnog," Gran'mon say. "Just keep that noise up."

"I want me some eggnog," I say; "and I 'tend to get me some eggnog tonight."

Next thing I know, Gran'mon done picked up a chip out o' that corner and done sailed it back there where me and Chuckkie is. I duck just in time, and the chip catch old Chuckkie side the head.

"Hey, who that hitting me?" Chuckkie say.

"Move, and you won't get hit," Gran'mon say.

I laugh at old Chuckkie over there holding his head, and next thing I know here's Chuckkie done haul back there and hit me in my side. I jump up from there and give him two just to show him how it feel, and he jump up and hit me again. Then we grab each other and start tussling on the floor.

"You, Ben O," I hear Gran'mon saying. "You, Ben O, cut that out. Y'all cut that out."

But we don't stop, 'cause neither one o' us want be first. Then I feel somebody pulling us apart.

"What I ought to do is whip both o' you," Mrs. Leola say. "Is that what y'all want?"

"No'm," I say.

"Then shake hand."

Me and Chuckkie shake hand.

"Kiss," Mrs. Leola say.

"No, ma'am," I say. "I ain't kissing no boy. I ain't that crazy."

"Kiss him, Chuckkie," she say.

Old Chuckkie kiss me on the jaw.

"Now, kiss him, Ben O."

"I ain't kissing no Chuckkie," I say. "No'm. Uh-uh. You kiss girls."

And the next thing I know, Mama done tipped up back o' me and done whop me on the leg with Daddy belt.

"Kiss Chuckkie," she say.

Chuckkie turn his jaw to me and I kiss him. I almost wipe my mouth. I even feel like spitting.

"Now, come back here and get you some eggnog," Mama say.

"That's right, spoil 'em," Gran'mon say. "Next thing you know, they be drinking from bottles."

"Little eggnog won't hurt 'em, Mama," Mama say.

"That's right, never listen," Gran'mon say. "It's you go'n suffer for it. I be dead and gone, me."

Aunt Clo

Be just like wrapping a chain round a tree and jecking and jecking, and then shifting the chain little bit and jecking and jecking some in that direction, and then shifting it some mo' and jecking and jecking in that direction. Jecking and jecking till you get it loose, and then pulling with all your might. Still it might not be loose enough and you have to back the tractor up some and fix the chain round the tree again and start jecking all over. Jeck, jeck, jeck. Then you hear the roots crying, and then you keep on jecking, and then it give, and you jeck some mo', and then it falls. And not till then that you see what you done done. Not till then you see the big hole in the ground and piece of the taproot still way down in it—a piece you won't never get out no matter if you dig till doomsday. Yes, you got the tree—least got it down on the ground, but did you get the taproot? No. No, sir, you didn't get the taproot. You stand there and look down in this hole at it and you grab yo' axe and jump down in it and start chopping at the taproot, but do you get the taproot? No. You don't get the taproot, sir. You never get the taproot. But, sir, I tell you what you do get. You get a big hole in the ground, sir; and you get another big hole in the air where the lovely branches been all these years. Yes, sir, that's what you get. The holes, sir, the holes. Two holes, sir, you can't never fill no matter how hard you try.

So you wrap yo' chain round yo' tree again, sir, and you start dragging it. But the dragging ain't so easy, sir, 'cause she's a heavy old tree—been there a long time, you know—heavy. And you make yo' tractor strain, sir, and the elements work 'gainst you, too, sir, 'cause the elements, they on her side, too, 'cause she part o' the elements, and the elements, they part o' her. So the elements, they do they little share to discourage you—yes, sir, they does. But you will not let the elements stop you. No, sir, you show the elements that they just elements, and man is stronger than elements, and you jeck and jeck on the chain, and soon she start to moving with you, sir, but if you look over yo' shoulder one second you see her leaving a trail—a trail, sir, that can be seen from miles and miles away. You see her trying to hook her little fine branches in different little cracks, in between pickets, round hills o' grass, round anything they might brush 'gainst. But you is a determined man, sir, and you jeck and you jeck, and she keep on grabbing and trying to hold, but you stronger, sir—course you the strongest—and you finally get her out on the pave road. But what you don't notice, sir, is just 'fore she get on the pave road she leave couple her little branches to remind the people that it ain't her that want leave, but you, sir, that think she ought to. So you just drag her and drag her, sir, and the folks that live in the houses 'side the pave road, they come out on they gallery and look at her go by, and then they go back in they house and sit by the fire and forget her. So you just go on, sir, and you just go and you go—and for how many days? I don't know. I don't have the least idea. The North to me, sir, is like the elements. It mystify me. But never mind, you finally get there, and then you try to find a place to set her. You look in this corner and you look in that corner, but no corner is good. She kind o' stand in the way no matter where you set her. So finally, sir, you say, "I just stand her up here a little while and see, and if it don't work out, if she keep getting in the way, I guess we'll just have to take her to the dump."

Chris

Just like him, though, standing up there telling them lies when everybody else feeling sad. I don't know what you do without people like him. And, yet, you see him there, he sad just like the rest. But he just got to be funny. Crying on the inside, but still got to be funny.

He didn't steal it, though; didn't steal it a bit. His grandpa was just like him. Mat? Mat Jefferson? Just like that. Mat could make you die laughing. 'Member once at a wake. Who was dead? Yes—Robert Lewis. Robert Lewis laying up in his coffin dead as a door nail. Everybody sad and droopy. Mat look at that and start his lying. Soon, half o' the place laughing. Funniest wake I ever went to, and yet—

Just like now. Look at 'em. Look at 'em laughing. Ten

minutes ago you would 'a' thought you was at a funeral. But look at 'em now. Look at her there in that little old chair. How long she had it? Fifty years—a hundred? It ain't a chair no mo', it's little bit o' her. Just like her arm, just like her leg.

You know, I couldn't believe it. I couldn't. Emile passed the house there the other day, right after the bombing, and I was in my yard digging a water drain to let the water run out in the ditch. Emile, he stopped the wagon there 'fore the door. Little Chuckkie, he in there with him with that little rain cap buckled up over his head. I go out to the gate and I say, "Emile, it's the truth?"

"The truth," he say. And just like that he say it. "The truth."

I look at him there, and he looking up the road to keep from looking back at me. You know, they been pretty close to Aunt Fe ever since they was children coming up. His own mon, Aunt Lou, and Aunt Fe, they been like sisters, there, together.

Me and him, we talk there little while 'bout the cane cutting, then he say he got to get on to the back. He shake the lines and drive on.

Inside me, my heart feel like it done swole up ten times the size it ought to be. Water come in my eyes, and I got to 'mit I cried right there. Yes sir, I cried right there by that front gate.

Louise come in the room and whisper something to Leola, and they go back in the kitchen. I can hear 'em moving things round back there, still getting things together they go'n be taking along. If they offer me anything, I'd like that big iron pot out there in the back yard. Good for boiling water when you killing hog, you know.

You can feel the sadness in the room again. Louise brought it in when she come in and whispered to Leola.

Only, she didn't take it out when her and Leola left. Every pan they move, every pot they unhook keep telling you she leaving, she leaving.

Etienne turn over one o' them logs to make the fire pick up some, and I see that boy, Lionel, spreading out his hands over the fire. Watch out, I think to myself, here come another lie. People, he just getting started.

Anne-Marie Duvall

"You're not going?"

"I'm not going," he says, turning over the log with the poker. "And if you were in your right mind, you wouldn't go, either."

"You just don't understand, do you?"

"Oh, I understand. She cooked for your daddy. She nursed you when your mama died."

"And I'm trying to pay her back with a seventy-nine-cents scarf. Is that too much?"

He is silent, leaning against the mantel, looking down at the fire. The fire throws strange shadows across the big, old room. Father looks down at me from against the wall. His eyes do not say go nor stay. But I know what he would do.

"Please go with me, Edward."

"You're wasting your breath."

I look at him a long time, then I get the small package from the coffee table.

"You're still going?"

"I am going."

"Don't call for me if you get bogged down anywhere back there."

I look at him and go out to the garage. The sky is black.

239

The clouds are moving fast and low. A fine drizzle is falling, and the wind coming from the swamps blows in my face. I cannot recall a worse night in all my life.

I hurry into the car and drive out of the yard. The house stands big and black in back of me. Am I angry with Edward? No, I'm not angry with Edward. He's right. I should not go out into this kind of weather. But what he does not understand is I must. Father definitely would have gone if he were alive. Grandfather definitely would have gone, also. And, therefore, I must. Why? I cannot answer why. Only, I must go.

As soon as I turn down that old muddy road, I begin to pray. Don't let me go into that ditch, I pray. Don't let me go into that ditch. Please, don't let me go into that ditch.

The lights play on the big old trees along the road. Here and there the lights hit a sagging picket fence. But I know I haven't even started yet. She lives far back into the fields. Why? God, why does she have to live so far back? Why couldn't she have lived closer to the front? But the answer to that is as hard for me as is the answer to everything else. It was ordained before I—before father—was born—that she should live back there. So why should I try to understand it now?

The car slides towards the ditch, and I stop it dead and turn the wheel, and then come back into the road again. Thanks, father. I know you're with me. Because it was you who said that I must look after her, didn't you? No, you did not say it directly, father. You said it only with a glance. As grandfather must have said it to you, and as his father must have said it to him.

But now that she's gone, father, now what? I know. I know. Aunt Lou, Aunt Clo, and the rest.

The lights shine on the dead, wet grass along the road. There's an old pecan tree, looking dead and all alone. I wish

I was a little nigger gal so I could pick pecans and eat them under the big old dead tree.

The car hits a rut, but bounces right out of it. I am frightened for a moment, but then I feel better. The windshield wipers are working well, slapping the water away as fast as it hits the glass. If I make the next half mile all right, the rest of the way will be good. It's not much over a mile now.

That was too bad about that bombing—killing that woman and her two children. That poor woman; poor children. What is the answer? What will happen? What do they want? Do they know what they want? Do they really know what they want? Are they positively sure? Have they any idea? Money to buy a car, is that it? If that is all, I pity them. Oh, how I pity them.

Not much farther. Just around that bend and—there's a water hole. Now what?

I stop the car and just stare out at the water a minute; then I get out to see how deep it is. The cold wind shoots through my body like needles. Lightning comes from towards the swamps and lights up the place. For a split second the night is as bright as day. The next second it is blacker than it has ever been.

I look at the water, and I can see that it's too deep for the car to pass through. I must turn back or I must walk the rest of the way. I stand there a while wondering what to do. Is it worth it all? Can't I simply send the gift by someone tomorrow morning? But will there be someone tomorrow morning? Suppose she leaves without getting it, then what? What then? Father would never forgive me. Neither would grandfather or great-grandfather, either. No, they wouldn't.

The lightning flashes again and I look across the field, and I can see the tree in the yard a quarter of a mile away. I have but one choice: I must walk. I get the package out of the car and stuff it in my coat and start out.

I don't make any progress at first, but then I become a little warmer and I find I like walking. The lightning flashes just in time to show up a puddle of water, and I go around it. But there's no light to show up the second puddle, and I fall flat on my face. For a moment I'm completely blind, then I get slowly to my feet and check the package. It's dry, not harmed. I wash the mud off my raincoat, wash my hands, and I start out again.

The house appears in front of me, and as I come into the yard, I can hear the people laughing and talking. Sometimes I think niggers can laugh and joke even if they see somebody beaten to death. I go up on the porch and knock and an old one opens the door for me. I swear, when he sees me he looks as if he's seen a ghost. His mouth drops open, his eyes bulge— I swear.

I go into the old crowded and smelly room, and every one of them looks at me the same way the first one did. All the joking and laughing has ceased. You would think I was the devil in person.

"Done, Lord," I hear her saying over by the fireplace. They move to the side and I can see her sitting in that little rocking chair I bet you she's had since the beginning of time. "Done, Master," she says. "Child, what you doing in weather like this? Y'all move; let her get to that fire. Y'all move. Move, now. Let her warm herself."

They start scattering everywhere.

"I'm not cold, Aunt Fe," I say. "I just brought you something—something small—because you're leaving us. I'm going right back."

"Done, Master," she says. Fussing over me just like she's done all her life. "Done, Master. Child, you ain't got no business in a place like this. Get close to this fire. Get here. Done, Master."

I move closer, and the fire does feel warm and good.

"Done, Lord," she says.

I take out the package and pass it to her. The other niggers gather around with all kinds of smiles on their faces. Just think of it—a white lady coming through all of this for one old darky. It is all right for them to come from all over the plantation, from all over the area, in all kinds of weather: this is to be expected of them. But a white lady, a white lady. They must think we white people don't have their kind of feelings.

She unwraps the package, her bony little fingers working slowly and deliberately. When she sees the scarf—the seventy-nine-cents scarf—she brings it to her mouth and kisses it.

"Y'all look," she says. "Y'all look. Ain't it the prettiest little scarf y'all ever did see? Y'all look."

They move around her and look at the scarf. Some of them touch it.

"I go'n put it on right now," she says. I go'n put it on right now, my lady."

She unfolds it and ties it round her head and looks up at everybody and smiles.

"Thank you, my lady," she says. "Thank you, ma'am, from the bottom of my heart."

"Oh, Aunt Fe." I say, kneeling down beside her. "Oh, Aunt Fe."

But I think about the other niggers there looking down at me, and I get up. But I look into that wrinkled old face again, and I must go back down again. And I lay my head in that bony old lap, and I cry and I cry—I don't know how long. And I feel those old fingers, like death itself, passing over my hair and my neck. I don't know how long I kneel there crying, and when I stop, I get out of there as fast as I can.

Etienne

The boy come in, and soon, right off, they get quiet, blaming the boy. If people could look little farther than the tip of they nose—No, they blame the boy. Not that they ain't behind the boy, what he doing, but they blame him for what she must do. What they don't know is that the boy didn't start it, and the people that bombed the house didn't start it, neither. It started a million years ago. It started when one man envied another man for having a penny mo' 'an he had, and then the man married a woman to help him work the field so he could get much 's the other man, but when the other man saw the man had married a woman to get much 's him, he, himself, he married a woman, too, so he could still have mo'. Then they start having children—not from love; but so the children could help 'em work so they could have mo'. But even with the children one man still had a penny mo' 'an the other, so the other man went and bought him a ox, and the other man did the same—to keep ahead of the other man. And soon the other man had bought him a slave to work the ox so he could get ahead of the other man. But the other man went out and bought him two slaves so he could stay ahead of the other man, and the other man went out and bought him three slaves. And soon they had a thousand slaves apiece, but they still wasn't satisfied. And one day the slaves all rose and kill the masters, but the masters (knowing slaves was men just like they was, and kind o' expected they might do this) organized theyself a good police force, and the police force, they come out and killed the two thousand slaves.

So it's not this boy you see standing here 'fore you, 'cause it happened a million years ago. And this boy here's just doing something the slaves done a million years ago. Just that this boy here ain't doing it they way. 'Stead of raising arms 'gainst the masters, he bow his head.

No, I say; don't blame the boy 'cause she must go. 'Cause when she's dead, and that won't be long after they get her up there, this boy's work will still be going on. She's not the only one that's go'n die from this boy's work. Many mo' of 'em go'n die 'fore it's over with. The whole place—everything. A big wind is rising, and when a big wind rise, the sea stirs, and the drop o' water you see laying on top the sea this day won't be there tomorrow. 'Cause that's what wind do, and that's what life is. She ain't nothing but one little drop o' water laying on top the sea, and what this boy's doing is called the wind . . . and she must be moved. No, don't blame the boy. Go out and blame the wind. No, don't blame him, 'cause tomorrow, what he's doing today, somebody go'n say he ain't done a thing. 'Cause tomorrow will he his time to be turned over just like it's hers today. And after that, be somebody else time to turn over. And it keep going like that till it ain't nothing left to turn—and nobody left to turn it.

"Sure, they bombed the house," he say; "because they want us to stop. But if we stopped today, then what good would we have done? What good? Those who have already died for the cause would have just died in vain."

"Maybe if they had bombed your house you wouldn't be so set on keeping this up."

"If they had killed my mother and my brothers and sisters, I'd press just that much harder. I can see you all point. I can see it very well. But I can't agree with you. You blame me for their being bombed. You blame me for Aunt Fe's leaving. They died for you and for your children. And I love Aunt Fe as much as anybody in here does. Nobody in here loves her more than I do. Not one of you." He looks at her. "Don't you believe me, Aunt Fe?"

She nods—that little white scarf still tied round her head.

"How many times have I eaten in your kitchen, Aunt Fe? A thousand times? How many times have I eaten tea cakes and drank milk on the back steps, Aunt Fe? A thousand times? How many times have I sat at this same fireplace with you, just the two of us, Aunt Fe? Another thousand times— two thousand times? How many times have I chopped wood for you, chopped grass for you, ran to the store for you? Five thousand times? How many times have we walked to church together, Aunt Fe? Gone fishing at the river together—how many times? I've spent as much time in this house as I've spent in my own. I know every crack in the wall. I know every corner. With my eyes shut, I can go anywhere in here without bumping into anything. How many of you can do that? Not many of you." He looks at her. "Aunt Fe?"

She looks at him.

"Do you think I love you, Aunt Fe?"

She nods.

"I love you, Aunt Fe, much as I do my own parents. I'm going to miss you much as I'd miss my own mother if she were to leave me now. I'm going to miss you, Aunt Fe, but I'm not going to stop what I've started. You told me a story once, Aunt Fe, about my great-grandpa. Remember? Remember how he died?"

She looks in the fire and nods.

"Remember how they lynched him—chopped him into pieces?"

She nods.

"Just the two of us were sitting here beside the fire when you told me that. I was so angry I felt like killing. But it was you who told me get killing out of my mind. It was you who told me I would only bring harm to myself and sadness to the others if I killed. Do you remember that, Aunt Fe?"

She nods, still looking in the fire.

"You were right. We cannot raise our arms. Because it would mean death for ourselves, as well as for the others. But we will do something else—and that's what we will do." He looks at the people standing round him. "And if they were to bomb my own mother's house tomorrow, I would still go on."

"I'm not saying for you not to go on," Louise says. "That's up to you. I'm just taking Auntie from here before hers is the next house they bomb."

The boy look at Louise, and then at Aunt Fe. He go up to the chair where she sitting.

"Good-bye, Aunt Fe," he say, picking up her hand. The hand done shriveled up to almost nothing. Look like nothing but loose skin's covering the bones. "I'll miss you," he say.

"Good-bye, Emmanuel," she say. She look at him a long time. "God be with you."

He stand there holding the hand a while longer, then he nods his head, and leaves the house. The people stir round little bit, but nobody say anything.

Aunt Lou

They tell her good-bye, and half of 'em leave the house crying, or want cry, but she just sit there 'side the fireplace like she don't mind going at all. When Leola ask me if I'm ready to go, I tell her I'm staying right there till Fe leave that house. I tell her I ain't moving one step till she go out that door. I been knowing her for the past fifty some years now, and I ain't 'bout to leave her on her last night here.

That boy, Chuckkie, want stay with me, but I make him go. He follow his mon and paw out the house and soon I hear that wagon turning round. I hear Emile saying something to Mr. Bascom even 'fore that wagon get out the yard. I tell myself, well, Mr. Bascom, you sure go'n catch it, and me not there to take up for you—and I get up from my chair and go to the door.

"Emile?" I call.

"Whoa," he say.

"You leave that mule 'lone, you hear me?"

"I ain't done Mr. Bascom a thing, Mama," he say.

"Well, you just mind you don't," I say. "I'll sure find out."

"Yes'm," he say. "Come up here, Mr. Bascom."

"Now, you hear that boy. Emile?" I say.

"I'm sorry, Mama," he say. "I didn't mean no harm."

They go out in the road, and I go back to the fireplace and sit down again. Louise stir round in the kitchen a few minutes, then she come in the front where we at. Everybody else gone. That husband o' hers, there, got drunk long 'fore midnight, and Emile and them had to put him to bed in the other room.

She come there and stand by the fire.

"I'm dead on my feet," she say.

"Why don't you go to bed," I say. "I'm go'n be here."

"You all won't need anything?"

"They got wood in that corner?"

"Plenty."

"Then we won't need a thing."

She stand there and warm, and then she say good night and go round the other side.

"Well, Fe?" I say.

"I ain't leaving here tomorrow, Lou," she say.

" 'Course you is," I say. "Up there ain't that bad."

She shake her head. "No, I ain't going nowhere."

I look at her over in her chair, but I don't say nothing.

The fire pops in the fireplace, and I look at the fire again. It's a good little fire—not too big, not too little. Just 'nough there to keep the place warm.

"You want sing, Lou?" she say, after a while. "I feel like singing my 'termination song."

"Sure," I say.

She start singing in that little light voice she got there, and I join with her. We sing two choruses, and then she stop.

"My 'termination for Heaven," she say. "Now—now—"

"What's the matter, Fe?" I say.

"Nothing," she say. "I want get in my bed. My gown hanging over there."

I get the gown for her and bring it back to the firehalf. She get out of her dress slowly, like she don't even have 'nough strength to do it. I help her on with her gown, and she kneel down there 'side the bed and say her prayers. I sit in my chair and look at the fire again.

She pray there a long time—half out loud, half to herself. I look at her kneeling down there, little like a little old girl. I see her making some kind o' jecking motion there, but I feel she crying 'cause this her last night here, and 'cause she got to go and leave ever'thing behind. I look at the fire.

She pray there ever so long, and then she start to get up. But she can't make it by herself. I go to help her, and when I put my hand on her shoulder, she say, "Lou? Lou?"

I say, "What's the matter, Fe?"

"Lou?" she say. "Lou?"

I feel her shaking in my hand with all her might. Shaking, shaking, shaking—like a person with the chill. Then I hear her take a long breath, longest I ever heard anybody take before. Then she ease back on the bed—calm, calm, calm.

"Sleep on, Fe," I tell her. "When you get up there, tell 'em all I ain't far behind."